W9-BEZ-057

ABOUT ISLAND PRESS

Island Press is the only nonprofit organization in the United States whose principal purpose is the publication of books on environmental issues and natural resource management. We provide solutions-oriented information to professionals, public officials, business and community leaders, and concerned citizens who are shaping responses to environmental problems.

Since 1984, Island Press has been the leading provider of timely and practical books that take a multidisciplinary approach to critical environmental concerns. Our growing list of titles reflects our commitment to bringing the best of an expanding body of literature to the environmental community throughout North America and the world.

Support for Island Press is provided by the Agua Fund, The Geraldine R. Dodge Foundation, Doris Duke Charitable Foundation, The Ford Foundation, The William and Flora Hewlett Foundation, The Joyce Foundation, Kendeda Sustainability Fund of the Tides Foundation, The Forrest & Frances Lattner Foundation, The Henry Luce Foundation, The John D. and Catherine T. MacArthur Foundation, The Marisla Foundation, The Andrew W. Mellon Foundation, Gordon and Betty Moore Foundation, The Curtis and Edith Munson Foundation, Oak Foundation, The Overbrook Foundation, The David and Lucile Packard Foundation, Wallace Global Fund, The Winslow Foundation, and other generous donors.

The opinions expressed in this book are those of the author(s) and do not necessarily reflect the views of these foundations.

PLANETIZEN CONTEMPORARY DEBATES IN URBAN PLANNING

PLANETIZEN CONTEMPORARY DEBATES IN URBAN PLANNING

Edited by

| Abhijeet Chavan | Christian Peralta | Christopher Steins |

 ISLANDPRESS   Washington | Covelo | London

Copyright © 2007 Urban Insight Inc.
Chapter 3.1, Planning For The Public Realm © Alexander Garvin

All rights reserved under International and Pan-American Copyright Conventions.
No part of this book may be reproduced in any form or by any means
without permission in writing from the publisher:
Island Press, Suite 300, 1718 Connecticut Ave., NW, Washington, DC 20009

Island Press is a trademark of the Center for Resource Economics.

Library of Congress Cataloging-in-Publication Data
Planetizen contemporary debates in urban planning/edited by Abhijeet Chavan,
Christian Peralta, Christopher Steins.
    p.   cm.
Includes index.
ISBN-13: 978-1-59726-132-6 (cloth : alk. paper)
ISBN-10: 1-59726-132-7 (cloth : alk. paper)
ISBN-13: 978-1-59726-133-3 (pbk. : alk. paper)
ISBN-10: 1-59726-133-5 (pbk. : alk. paper)
1. Cities and towns—United States—Growth. 2. City planning—United States.
3. Regional planning—United States. 4. Mixed-use developments—United States.
5. Sustainable development—United States.
I. Chavan, Abhijeet. II. Peralta, Christian. III. Steins, Christopher.
HT384.U5P53 2007
307.1'216—dc22
2006100958

Printed on recycled, acid-free paper ♲

Manufactured in the United States of America

10 9 8 7 6 5 4 3 2 1

Keywords: Land use planning, sprawl, transportation,
suburb, architecture, gentrification, disaster planning,
housing, eminent domain.

TABLE OF CONTENTS

FOREWORD | Neal Peirce

Pendulums swing. But how rapidly and how far? That's what this book of fascinating opinion pieces on American growth is all about.

We all know the pendulum swung greatly in America from 1945 into the 1990s. The United States experienced one of the most exuberant periods of growth any civilization has ever seen—world-dominating industrialization, financial leadership, and entertainment-based cultural exports all burst onto the global scene.

One characteristic of this particular pendulum swing was a historically unprecedented, distinctive form of land settlement—the phenomenon we called suburbanization. From Levittown forward, the dream of one's own home on a fresh piece of land propelled the movement. The driving factors included massive federal road building and subsidies to suburban home owners, mass-produced automobiles, cheap energy (I can remember 18-cents-a-gallon gas in the 1950s!), lagging urban schools, and middle-class fears of inner-city crime or racial divides. Freeway and auto mobility fed a whole new form of retailing, from the early malls to battalions of Wal-Marts popping up beside smaller cities nationwide and undermining their Main Streets' viability. Not accidentally, by 1990 more Americans lived in suburbia than in center cities and rural areas combined.

Then, in the 1990s, came New Urbanism—a new and innovative architectural form and lifestyle model. It represented the first alternative to the standard suburban model that Americans had seen in decades. The movement evoked images of friendlier, more intimate and walkable towns and neighborhoods and, by extension, less dependence on automobiles and the country's increasingly congested, polluted highways. The smart growth movement followed soon after, articulating goals of a radically less land- and energy-consumptive society, fighting sterile zoning rules, and opposing the superroads and big box retailing. By 2000, the most significant "return to city" movement since World War II was underway.

Call this most recent movement, if you will, a signal that the pendulum might be ready to swing back to traditional towns and cities. But did the pendulum really ever change direction? *Should it?*

Planetizen (an interactive Web site, itself a radical new form of communication; see www.planetizen.com) picked up this critical issue in 2000, providing an instant forum for the lively exchange of ideas by people inside, and by outsiders looking into, urban planning in America. This book, with entries ranging back to the start of the decade and including brand-new material, provides a rich array of competing, clashing, and on occasion surprisingly compatible prescriptions and predictions on how the country is growing, its real choices, and the ideological and economic choices it faces.

I'm intrigued when journalist Anthony Flint celebrates smart growth but confesses that *affordability* of housing is the key question of its future (chapter 1.1). Or when Michael Mehaffy, project manager during the critical building years of Portland's pathbreaking transit-oriented development (TOD) at Orenco Station, not only celebrates the project's diversity and pedestrian-friendly street design but notes hard lessons learned (chapter 2.5). Among Mehaffy's pieces of advice to transit-oriented development (TOD) makers: remember that density demands fine design, but let it evolve; learn to cope with the diseconomies of mixed-use construction; create a team of supporters ranging from elected officials down to desk clerks, along with skilled private consultants; and deal with the challenge, in today's real estate market, of creating housing that includes options for low- or moderate-income buyers.

If you like ingenious ideas on how cities can work better, don't miss Kenneth Kruckemeyer's captivating description of Bogotá's car-free Sunday mornings and his resourceful prescriptions for weaning ourselves, if ever so mildly, from the roadway monopoly of "automobilization" (chapter 2.4), or Donald Shoup's suggestions on how to charge users what street parking is *really* worth, using the proceeds for such needed services as cleaning streets, planting trees, improving lighting, and removing graffiti (chapter 2.2).

Other chapters are just as inventive: Dan Burden's ten keys to truly walkable communities (chapter 2.1); Peter Samuel's musings on the potential of variable tolls on major highways (charged electronically, adjusted by hour and congestion level; see chapter 2.3); Jeff Speck's imaginative but practical raft of city design resolutions based on the rich experience base of the Mayors' Institute on City Design (Chapter 3.2); and Constance Beaumont's powerful rationale for favoring community-centered schools in place of the oversized edge-of-town schools swimming in asphalt (Chapter 5.4). The reader can also expore *Kelo* and eminent domain, the real or exaggerated dangers of gentrification, deciding how much to rebuild (or not rebuild) water-imperiled New Orleans, and many other topics, and be promised few dull moments.

But it's the pendulum swing, explicit or tucked away between the lines of these essays and spirited rejoinders, that makes this book exceptional. Are we at the threshold of—indeed, already embarked on—a historic turn toward more compact communities and traditional urbanism? Will the pendulum at least begin to inch back to the more historic form of cities? Or has the suburban model of automobile-enabled low urban densities, enforced by zoned separate residential-commercial-office uses, become so dominant in Americans' preferences, so ingrained in the United States' economic model, that today's notions of New Urbanism, smart growth, and mixed-use development are destined for oblivion? Will the pendulum of heavily dispersed American development continue its momentum largely unrestrained?

Or are we headed toward the middle of the arc: a hybrid form of compact and dispersed forms intermingling based on diversified markets, tastes, incomes, and ethnic mixes?

Most of us are likely to guess the future based on our individual preferences—what we'd *prefer* to see occur. And surely, whatever your preferences may be, you'll find at least one writer in this collection whose outlook makes you exclaim, "That's it. Right on!"

Let me be honest about my own view. I believe the harsh realities of the twenty-first-century world will wrench us Americans off the global comfort seat made possible by our current standard of living, produced by our global military superiority, and enabled by our dispersed physical form of development.

The first big reason is energy. Our massive auto and truck fleets, traveling mind-numbing cumulative distances over our dispersed patterns of settlement, gorge on liquid fuel. They guzzle so much that we're now dependent on foreign sources for more than 60 percent of our oil, an important part of the supply coming from countries susceptible to rapid and potentially violent political change, such as Venezuela, Nigeria, and Saudi Arabia. U.S. domestic "finds" will provide only a temporary new supply. We *know* oil prices will escalate well beyond today's figures, especially with India and China pushing aggressively and competitively into the world oil market. Gas at $3 a gallon? Think $8 or $10 in a few years. Oil at $70 a barrel? Think $100, perhaps $200, very soon.

And with those thoughts in mind, consider how a global energy supply crisis, triggered by terrorist attacks, weather-related disasters, or simply a pattern of ever-diminished supply, would bring our traffic flows to near standstill, crippling our metropolitan economies. And *then* talk about a "new suburbanism."

The second reason is global warming. We're burning a quarter of the world's fossil fuels and emitting a like percentage of greenhouse gases into the atmosphere. The perils to the livability of the planet are becoming more vivid and irrefutable, as repeated scientific studies underscore the growing danger. Unless the United States, as the prime polluter, takes leadership, there will be no way to convince developing nations to seek and implement the radical carbon-saving steps necessary to meet their explosive new energy demand without dire peril to their climate, their lands, their future as societies. For the first time in world history, a single issue is threatening human civilization as a whole. The United States will be unable to reduce its huge carbon footprint without embracing radically more compact styles of human settlement.

Third, as a nation, we're failing at basic investments in infrastructure repair and improvement. We're already far behind in updating the aging road and water systems built in the decades after World War II. The experts predict the catch-up will cost us hundreds of billions, perhaps trillions, of dollars. In new infrastructure, we're falling rapidly behind new world standards: fourteen nations around the globe, for example, are now building intercity rapid rail systems with top speeds of more than two hundred miles per hour. If our new mode has to be playing catch-up, how can we afford the infrastructure for continuing new waves of sprawling development?

Finally, we have a national government sunk deep into debt, spending like a drunken sailor even as the demographic tsunami of the aging baby boomers gets ready to crest. Simultaneously, we've engaged in a bellicose national foreign policy, symbolized by the Iraq war and deepening global hostilities toward us.

I believe we had an opportunity, following the fall of the Berlin Wall and even after 9/11, to mount an imaginative, first-ever-in-history effort by a superpower to use its capital, its technology, and its environmental expertise to lift up standards of living and sustainable agendas across the globe.

Inventing and building creative and ecologically sustainable new human communities here, while making their technology available across the globe, could have become a great American mission. Instead, we lapsed into the kinds of power plays and idle use of wealth and foreign military adventures that have brought empires to their knees since the dawn of time.

My bottom line is that we'll be extraordinarily lucky if we can simply make up for lost ground—solidify our existing cities and metropolitan regions, recapture our brownfields and dead big boxes, remake our commercial strips into habitable boulevards, redesign our water and power systems and sprawl-imperiled farm fields for enhanced local self-sufficiency, and apply our intelligence to create conserving and sustainable neighborhoods and cities for this century.

But even if you disagree, don't despair—not just yet, anyway. This book, packed with lively commentary, will let your mind voyage and discover as it will and leave no facile assumption unchallenged.

—NEAL PEIRCE

ACKNOWLEDGMENTS

Planetizen is first and foremost an online community. The active participation of this community is what powers Planetizen and has helped us to grow. We would like to thank all Planetizen readers and volunteer correspondents for their support, feedback, and ideas.

We would also like to thank the authors who have contributed to this book for their enthusiastic involvement at such short notice. We owe special thanks to Neal Peirce for graciously writing the foreword to this volume. We would also like to thank Paul Zykofsky and Nancy Mathison of the Local Government Commission, and Ryan Armstrong from the Orange County Transportation Authority, for their assistance with artwork.

Planetizen is a team effort, and we would like to recognize the key role our colleagues have played in bringing this project to fruition. Former Managing Editor David Gest laid the foundation for this book's structure. Assistant Editor Nate Berg's organization and energy propelled the project. Art Director Mindy Oliver's wizardry with pixels made the visuals in this book possible. Senior Web Developer Michael Jelks's programming expertise keeps the Planetizen website humming. Office Manager Brenda Meyer, our resident expert on publishing, guided us through the process and kept the project on track.

Finally, we would like to thank Shannon O'Neill, Heather Boyer, and the entire team at Island Press for making this book a reality. We know we presented them with many challenges. But Island Press was always able to find a way to make our unusual ideas possible. We admire their flexibility and their invaluable guidance.

INTRODUCTION

The scales have tipped. We now live in a time when the majority of the world's population lives in cities. This historic milestone both highlights the astonishing success of human civilization and draws more attention to the glaring problems faced by urbanized society. Above all, it has strengthened the role of urban planning as a discipline in creating strategies that encourage the continued development of urban areas in ways that allow the residents to live full, healthy, and productive lives.

The history of directing the physical layout of cities goes back thousands of years. The great cities of ancient civilizations in Europe, Asia, the Middle East, and the Americas are all examples of deliberately planned human settlements—some with remarkable complexity. Yet, urban planning as a modern discipline can also be considered a new endeavor, with its origins in the desire to rationalize the growth of cities during the industrialization of the nineteenth century. Since then, the practice of planning has been in constant flux, changing to respond to our growing understanding of how cities function and the impact they have on our society, the economy, and the natural environment.

In 2000, we created the Planetizen website (www.planetizen.com) to provide a forum for communication, debate, and dialogue in the fields of urban planning, design, and development. The news and commentary that we have published over the years—covering many major trends in the field from a wide range of perspectives—have been well received. Both established experts and some new voices have been eager to share their ideas with our growing audience of people interested in the future of cities. And thanks to the power of the Internet, our readers have been equally able to share their thoughts, creating a ongoing discussion among professionals and nonprofessionals from across the country and around the world.

Having had the privilege of hosting some of the most fascinating, perceptive, and sometimes controversial opinions about urban planning on Planetizen, we hoped to gather some of the most insightful commentaries, along with selected reader comments, in one place for the benefit of readers. This volume is the result of that desire. Combined with a number of new articles from leading thinkers, this collection represents our attempt to provide a thorough (but by no means authoritative) overview of the intellectual debate that has occurred in the fields of urban planning, design, and development in recent years.

We hope that the ideas included in this collection will help inform and inspire those seeking to help create new places to live, work, and play—be it one neighborhood block or an entire region. The diversity of people and places in this world ensures that there is no one answer that can solve the problems that face cities. Continually examining ideas—both new and old—will always be an essential condition if we have any chance of meeting the challenge of an increasingly urbanized globe. As the fields of urban planning and development enter a critical and exciting new era, we look forward eagerly to the work of providing an open, visible forum for the profound debates that will ultimately help shape our cities.

SPRAWL VS. SMART GROWTH
Introduction by the Editors of Planetizen

If there is one dynamic that has characterized urban planning and development over the last fifty years, it has been the transformation of our cities from traditionally compact, dense, urban centers to the dispersed, multicentered metropolises of today. This paradigm shift, largely brought about by the democratization and widespread adoption of the automobile, has fundamentally altered how cities look and function in the twenty-first century. Suburban housing tracts, office parks, shopping malls, and the roads and highways that connect them became the primary building blocks of urban planners who sought to build cities that delivered on the promise of the fabled American dream.

More than fifty years after the suburban revolution, the planning profession has arrived at a crossroads. While Americans have largely enjoyed unprecedented prosperity during the period of suburbanization, continued growth has created many challenges for cities. Chief among these growing problems is traffic congestion. Along with a dramatic decrease in mobility, the clogged roads and highways have contributed to an increase in air pollution. In addition, concerns ranging from the dwindling supply of land for housing, the loss of agricultural land and open space, increasing economic inequality and social isolation, and even the growing epidemic of obesity have been blamed on the typical landscape of urban sprawl and the suburban lifestyle it supports.

As a solution to these problems, a growing number of urban planners and designers have begun to advocate new ways to develop, and many are looking to the smart growth movement. Smart growth advocates for land use patterns that encourage walking, biking, and the use of transit, that are more compact, and that offer a mix of residential and commercial uses. Supporters of smart growth assert that by using land more efficiently (increasing density); building homes, offices, stores, and parks within close proximity to one another (mixing uses); and linking development with transportation infrastructure, cities can continue to accommodate growth without creating the negative impacts associated with urban sprawl.

Over the past decade, the smart growth movement has become more and more accepted by planners and local officials seeking to counter some of the consequences of conventional suburban development. Further, since the tenets of smart growth include the redirection of public investment away from the suburbs to central cities, the preservation of farmland and open space, and a reduction of car use in favor of public transit, the movement has gained allies outside the planning profession, among the environmental and social justice advocates working to protect wilderness and revive the inner cities of American metropolises. This mounting support for smart growth has helped produce a growing number of model developments and has begun to encourage some cities to reorient their planning policies in line with the philosophy of smart growth.

However, smart growth's prescription is not popular with everyone. Nor is fitting more people into less space and getting them to ride transit easy to accomplish. As the smart growth movement has gained prominence, a growing number of opponents—including market-oriented economists, anti-regulatory Libertarians, and many longtime residents of established urban and suburban communities—have decried the smart growth movement for its "coercion" of the urban landscape against the wishes of the public.

One major obstacle for smart growth is increasing density. Although planners and officials cite that dense, compact cities can use land more efficiently and offer walkability, it seems that the majority of Americans still prefer living in detached, single-family homes in low-density communities (and indeed most do). Whether this preference is real or perceived is a hotly debated issue. Sprawl defenders argue that the market has provided what the American public has demanded, while smart growth supporters claim that the regulatory framework of zoning codes has made it nearly impossible to provide any alternatives. Adding to the problem is the negative image of dense urban areas, seen as cesspools of poverty and crime, in the minds of many Americans. Some studies cited by smart growth opponents also suggest that higher-density development increases both traffic congestion (and therefore toxic emissions) and housing prices—two things that smart growth claims to ameliorate.

By its own admission, the smart growth movement has been doggedly tailed by the problem of housing affordability. Subsidies have often been required to create many of the most celebrated examples of transit-oriented development, and most urban housing tends to cost more than its counterparts in the suburbs. However, an increasing number of housing experts agree that the days of the cheap house in the suburbs are also ending. After fifty years of suburban growth, most of the land around cities has been blanketed with homes, and the supply of land available for the development of new suburbs is rapidly dwindling. And although urban housing may cost a little more, supporters cite the significant savings that urban dwellers can achieve in lower transportation costs once they are liberated from commuting long distances.

In addition to density, the other major issue in the debate over urban sprawl and smart growth is the role of the automobile. Although cars once provided seemingly unlimited mobility, road and highway construction has not kept pace. Rather than invest in road construction, smart growth advocates want to encourage more people to use public transit. Yet most people agree that the state of public transit in all but a few American cities is woefully inadequate and inefficient, if not completely absent. Whereas supporters of smart growth see this as a call for greater investment in public transit systems, opponents consistently point out that the U.S. transit industry has spent hundreds of billions of dollars building rail transit systems over the past several decades, with little impact on the transportation habits of most Americans. Critics of smart growth also point out that traditional public transit is ill-suited to the commuting patterns of the modern economy, in which employment is dispersed around a region.

The lack of a clear definition of what actually constitutes smart growth is another obstacle. Some communities use smart growth as a tool to prevent any new development, while some enterprising housing developers have used smart growth as a guise to fit more homes in a typical suburban subdivision. For those communities that have made a commitment to smart growth policies, the legacy of urban sprawl is proving difficult to retrofit—lack of street connectivity and public transit access pose major challenges to densification.

Even with all these obstacles, smart growth holds much promise for many urban areas that have exhausted their capacity to support low-density development and are seeking new ways to accommodate growth without exacerbating the problems typically associated with new development. These proving grounds will be crucial for the mainstream adoption of smart growth policies.

Today, the battle over sprawl and smart growth rages on in the nation's cities and neighborhoods. With growing awareness of the environmental and geopolitical consequences of the typical American lifestyle, more and more Americans are beginning to seek a more sustainable lifestyle. If able to deliver on its promises, smart growth could be instrumental in the creation of a new American dream—one that perhaps features an urban flat in a neighborhood where everything is within walking distance.

A TIPPING POINT—BUT NOW THE HARD PART

Anthony Flint |

Smart growth is clearly making headway in urban areas across the country, but much remains to be done if the trend is to be sustained. Housing affordability ranks first among the challenges waiting to be tackled.

A funny thing has happened on the way to the revolution. Smart growth, New Urbanism, green building, and more sustainable development have all been trying to push their way into the American consciousness. Now that energy and transportation costs have soared, and the realities of global warming and energy dependence have truly sunk in, these practices are rather in vogue as a matter of consumer preference.

Leave it to the American consumer to snap to attention: understanding the real costs of living in sprawl, appreciating a more "right-sized" life in which it's possible to walk to a corner store or hop on a trolley, and grasping how a good city park can be just as good as, or better than, a football field–size backyard. Now the builders of mixed-use, more concentrated, transit-oriented, and sustainable communities are rushing to meet a new demand, and single-family homes in subdivisions are not quite so popular. Toll Brothers and KB Homes, for example, saw massive earnings declines—and many of the large corporate homebuilders hastily established higher-density units. Owners of McMansions slashed prices and tossed in flat-screen TVs. A shift is clearly underway, as projects from Atlantic Station in Atlanta to warehouse renovations in downtown Minneapolis have filled up.

Yet, advocates of smart growth, New Urbanism, and sustainable development face new and greater challenges. The work that remains to be done includes convincing more local and state governments to tackle zoning and code reform and to shift investments and policies to support transit, more concentrated development, and revitalization in cities, town centers, and older suburbs. Now is also the time for more thoughtful long-range and regional planning in the arrangement of housing and jobs. Perhaps most important of all, these new, more sustainable patterns must be made affordable to the widest range of American families.

Affordability is a big part of the engine that drove sprawl in the first place, along with a quest for wide-open spaces, backyards and patios, good schools, and especially since September 11, a sense of safety and security to raise our families. In researching my book, *This Land: The Battle over Sprawl and the Future of America* (Baltimore: Johns Hopkins University Press, 2006), I visited Little Elm, Texas, a boomtown north of Dallas, where the homes started at $100,000. Across the country, home buyers "drive to qualify"—driving as far as needed to get to the subdivision house they can afford, even if it's two hours from where they work. This dynamic is at work in West Virginia, the new bedroom community for the Washington, D.C., area; in California's Central Valley, the new commuter shed for San Jose, Oakland, and San Francisco; and in Worcester County in my home state of Massachusetts, where Christmas tree farms and summer camps are being turned into subdivisions. As one woman told a *Boston Globe* real estate reporter recently, she's willing to drive three hours a day "if I can come home to a castle" (Joan Axelrod-Contrada, "Westward Home; Buyers Find a Price They Can Pay and Some Breathing Room, if They Can Bear the Commute," *The Boston Globe*, April 9, 2006).

But affordability is also going to be a major force behind the new paradigm—the shift to more concentrated settlement patterns. With the cost of energy and transportation factored in, sprawl isn't the bargain it's cracked up to be. Those long commutes mean $70 or $100 a week to fill up the tank. Annually, the cost of owning and operating a car is creeping up to $10,000 a year—easily worth $100,000 on a mortgage. The bills for heating and cooling large homes are also weighing heavily on the family budget.

It's no mystery, then, why demand is increasing for alternatives. The big question is whether government is ready to smooth the way for these alternatives, by overhauling the system of rules, subsidies, and investment needs, starting with zoning. The current rules make it difficult to build compact, concentrated, and urban infill redevelopment. Eighty-year-old zoning requires dispersal and forbids mixed use. It actually limits housing choices.

Zoning and code reform is at the top of the to-do list, but other policies and incentives also need to change. Michigan, Pennsylvania, and Massachusetts have instituted a "Fix It First" policy that prioritizes the repair of existing transportation infrastructure, whether roads or transit, before any new sprawl-enabling highways are built.

Massachusetts, while under Republican Governor Mitt Romney, also changed the way state funding for local infrastructure is distributed, through a smart growth "scorecard" that rewards communities that increase housing production in smart locations. Cities and towns get cash incentives for dense residential development in town centers and downtowns, on vacant industrial land, or near transit. About $30 million was made available for transit-oriented development, supporting some eighty projects representing twenty-five thousand new homes that are proposed, under construction, or already built. A smart growth tool kit helped cities and towns use different techniques to change local land use policy, whether the transfer of development rights or new bylaws to legalize accessory apartments. A new highway design manual jettisons minimum width and design requirements and instead encourages attractive, multiuse, traffic-calmed main streets for town centers and downtowns. New standards for energy efficiency through green building practices, starting with school buildings and public libraries, are also on the way.

All of these policies changed the DNA of development. But the work doesn't end there. Arguably the hardest task ahead is to make sure all of this new growth, as well as revitalized cities and older suburbs, is affordable.

The worst possible outcome would be for middle-class families to be squeezed from both ends—in other words, when they look for alternatives to increasingly budget-busting sprawl, they find only gentrified urban neighborhoods or pricey transit-oriented or New Urbanist developments. There is a ready audience here. Of all of life's challenges, human habitat in the U.S. today is driving the middle class crazy.

Zoning reform and new development policies will help solve part of this problem by increasing supply. Compared to the amount of sprawl, very few revitalized urban neighborhoods or New Urbanist project exist. If there could be more of them—if smart growth could be as ubiquitous as sprawl—the laws of supply and demand would take over and they wouldn't be so expensive. The range of housing types that smart growth provides is also, by definition, an expansion of affordability.

Other interventions and techniques also address affordability, however, and that's where much of the ferment and energy and experimentation is today. Inclusionary zoning requires 10 or 15 percent of new development to be affordable, either on-site or off-site. Linkage programs establish affordable housing trust funds to which developers contribute. Under the density bonus model, developers can build more homes if they provide a larger affordable component. Increasingly popular community benefit agreements, in which developers negotiate a package of neighborhood amenities and benefits that accompany projects, invariably include an affordability component.

Community land trusts—where the cost of the land is taken out of the home-buying equation—are catching on across the country, from Irvine, California, to Chicago, Illinois; Austin, Texas; and Delray Beach, Florida. The Lincoln Institute of Land Policy in Cambridge, Massachusetts, is doing extensive research on community land trusts, and what works and what doesn't.

The design world is pitching in as well. We're finally paying attention to well-designed, affordable housing the way we once figured out how to make a sleek, inexpensive car. For example, the hurricanes of 2005 produced the Katrina cottage, which can be built inexpensively (and added on to) to replace FEMA trailers.

All across the country, Americans are turning from sprawl and discovering the benefits of living in walkable, mixed-use environments, close to parks, stores, and transit. Urbanism is being recognized as an amenity—something that adds value for everybody. It's better for the planet to live this way, but it's also more satisfying at a personal level. That's a powerful combination.

The smart growth movement has gone from preaching about the wastefulness of sprawl to simply providing what more people want. The rules need to be changed so that alternatives to sprawl can exist. And affordability can't be an add-on—it has to be part and parcel of this new paradigm. If such implementation can be done right, this could be smart growth's finest hour.

ANTHONY FLINT

is a former reporter for *The Boston Globe* and the author of *This Land: The Battle Over Sprawl and the Future of America*, published in April 2006 by Johns Hopkins University Press. He is currently public affairs manager for the Lincoln Institute of Land Policy, a think tank based in Cambridge, Massachusetts, where he continues to write about land and development. His forthcoming book on Jane Jacobs and Robert Moses in New York in the 1960s will be published in 2008 by Random House.

THE ARGUMENT AGAINST SMART GROWTH

Wendell Cox

Does smart growth result in more traffic congestion and air pollution? Wendell Cox presents the argument against smart growth.

Over the past sixty years, America's suburbs have grown to contain most urban residents. As the nation has become more affluent, people have chosen to live in single-family dwellings on individual lots and have also obtained automobiles to provide unprecedented mobility.

As the population has continued to grow, the amount of new roadway constructed has fallen far short of the rise in automobile use. As a result, American urban areas are experiencing increased traffic congestion. The good news is that improved vehicle technology has made the air cleaner in many cities than it has been in decades.

Low-density suburbanization is perceived by the antisprawl movement as inefficiently using land by consuming open space and valuable agricultural land. The antisprawl movement believes that suburbanization has resulted in an inappropriate amount of automobile use and highway construction and favors public transit and walking as alternatives. Moreover, it blames suburbanization for the decline of the nation's central cities.

The antisprawl movement has embraced "smart growth" policies. In general, smart growth would increase urban population densities, especially in corridors served by rail transit. Development would be corralled within urban growth boundaries. There would be little or no highway construction, replaced instead by construction of urban rail systems. Attempts would be made to steer development toward patterns that would reduce home-to-work travel distances, making transit and walking more feasible. The antisprawl movement suggests that these policies would improve quality of life while reducing traffic congestion and air pollution.

But the antisprawl diagnosis is flawed.

- *Urbanization does not threaten agricultural land.* Since 1950, urban areas of more than 1 million in population have consumed an amount of new land equal to barely one-tenth of the area taken out of agricultural production. The culprit is improved agricultural productivity, not development.

- *Only 15 percent of suburban growth has come from declining central cities.* Most growth is simple population gain and the movement of people from rural to suburban areas. The same process is occurring throughout affluent nations of Europe, Asia, and Australia. In these regions, virtually all urban growth in recent decades has been suburban, while central cities have lost population. Since 1950, Copenhagen has lost 40 percent of its population and Paris 25 percent.

- *There is no practical way for low-density urban areas to be redesigned to significantly increase transit and walking.* Whether in the United States or Europe, most urban destinations are reasonably accessible only by automobile. Transit can be an effective alternative to the automobile only to dense core areas, such as the nation's largest downtowns.

- *Large expanses of land are already protected as open space.* All of the nation's urban development, in small towns and major metropolitan areas, accounts for approximately 4 percent of land (excluding Alaska).

  Ironically, smart growth will bring more traffic congestion and air pollution because it will concentrate automobile traffic in a smaller geographical space. International and U.S. data show that

  - higher population densities are associated with greater traffic congestion

  - the slower, more stop-and-go traffic caused by higher densities increases air pollution.

Further, urban growth boundaries ration land for development. Rationing, whether of gasoline or land, drives prices up. For example, in smart growth–oriented Portland, Oregon, housing affordability has declined considerably more than in any other major metropolitan area. This makes it unnecessarily difficult for low-income and many minority citizens to purchase their own homes.

The antisprawl movement has not identified any threat that warrants its Draconian policies. As the "Lone Mountain Compact" (see chapter 5.5) puts it, people should be allowed to live and work where and how they like, absent a material threat to others.

As urban areas continue to expand—which they must do in a growing affluent nation—sufficient street and highway capacity should be provided so that traffic congestion and air pollution are minimized.

WENDELL COX

---

is principal of Wendell Cox Consultancy, an international public policy firm. He has provided consulting assistance to the United States Department of Transportation and is a visiting professor at the Conservatoire National des Arts et Metiers in Paris. He has consulted for public transit authorities in the United States, Canada, Australia, and New Zealand and for public policy organizations.

This article was originally published by Planetizen on January 22, 2001.

RESPONSES FROM READERS

Missing the Bigger Picture

Mr. Cox's arguments against the antisprawl movement (anti-antisprawl) hold on a macro level but miss the point overall.

Yes, agricultural yields have increased, but sprawl consumes prime farmland. Many major urban areas developed around farming centers; the loss of prime land means agriculture requires more artificial means to sustain increasing yields. The United States is a huge landmass, so any measure of gain or loss of lands to various uses appears insignificant when taken as a whole. A city-by-city analysis reveals a much different picture. Metropolitan Cleveland, Chicago, Philadelphia, Detroit, and other cities lost population for decades after 1950, while their suburban areas expanded. Metro population growth resulted more from the shift from city to suburb than from real growth. *Sprawl* and *growth* are not synonymous.

Further, while higher densities are required to support transit and offer choices of how and where to work and live, smart growth does not suggest that all development be of equal density. The highest densities should focus on the one-quarter- to one-half-mile radii surrounding transit stops. At three-quarters of a mile, few people will walk to a station, suggesting a lowering of densities with distance from a station.

Transit can reduce automobile trips, as confirmed by conservative writers Paul M. Weyrich and William S. Lind (*Does Transit Work? A Conservative Reappraisal*, Free Congress Foundation, October 2003). Whereas only 3 to 4 percent of all trips are by transit nationally, approximately 50 percent of trips into Chicago's Loop occur by transit, with higher figures for New York, of course. Safe, convenient public transit to a central location works; if more jobs returned to central cities, transit would be even more effective.

But what amount of street/highway construction would be effective? The Surface Transportation Policy Project reported in 1999 that regions where road building kept pace with population growth experienced just as much congestion as did regions where road building declined on a per capita basis. This suggests that regions cannot build their way out of congestion; in fact, new roads lead to induced demand.

One should also note that very few states or regions have adopted or will adopt urban growth boundaries. Most smart growth policy initiatives simply call for focusing infrastructure spending in existing communities, rather than reaching out to foster further sprawl. We are in little danger of running out of land available for development or growth.

Finally, housing costs have increased in Portland, yes, but also in sprawling areas such as Salt Lake City. Portland attracts new employment, and along with its new employees, some of whom aren't yet ready to buy housing: of course, homeownership will decline as a percentage . . . but providing low-income housing requires a number of approaches, none of which requires sprawl as an outcome.

The smart growth or antisprawl movement does not restrict choice in how we live: it requires communities to provide more choices than one-size-fits-all suburbanization.   —*January 24, 2001*

Do We Even Need Smart Growth?

Here in Lincoln, Nebraska—a university town—we constantly hear the drumbeat for smart growth. However, absent smart growth policies, 90 percent of our county population is already housed on 8 percent of the land in Lancaster County. You can't get much smarter growth than that. The resulting density per square mile is slightly greater than Portland, Oregon. For us to try to institute mass transit would be unworkable because like most areas of the country, you have to have "mass" before you can have mass transit.   —*January 25, 2001*

Weak Prosprawl Arguments

As smart growth and New Urbanism gain momentum, a small number of apologists try to justify the mess that sixty years of mass suburbanization has brought. In the typical fashion, Mr. Cox has delivered a defense full of falsehoods and weak arguments.

First of all, one of the largest falsehoods is that mass suburbanization happened by accident, by the will of the free market. In reality, sprawl has been heavily subsidized while traditional urbanism has been practically outlawed in most of the country. FHA mortgages that could be used only for new suburban homes, massive highway building and neglect of transit, urban renewal policies that killed cities, and low gas taxes compared to Europe made sprawl possible. Without these and other government policies, it would be impossible to house a majority of our population this way.

One of the biggest factors, however, is zoning. By requiring large lots, the separation of housing types, and the separation of land uses, zoning makes traditional urbanism illegal. Anyone attempting to build dense, mixed-use, walkable urbanism will be shot down by most municipalities in the nation.

What happens when a developer is able to get a traditional, nonsprawl project built? Usually it sells like hotcakes, that's what! In Sacramento, a downtown infill project with a density of twenty units to the acre, called "Metro Square," sold out in one day. Real estate analysts in Maryland studying the Kentlands, a New Urbanist project, said that if a home were moved from the surrounding sprawl subdivisions into the Kentlands neighborhood it would gain $35,000 in value that day. This stuff sells. Does everyone want to live this way? No. But should it be illegal? Certainly not. Market surveys show that approximately 30 percent of home buyers would like to buy a home in a New Urbanist project. With this style of development outlawed in most of the country, most of these home buyers have to settle for a typical subdivision.

Another of Mr. Cox's weak arguments claims that higher densities bring traffic congestion. That may be true if the higher densities are laid out in a suburban fashion with segregated land uses and a disconnected street pattern. But if the higher densities are laid out in a traditional urban fashion with mixed uses and a connected grid of streets, then this is absolutely false. I visited Orenco Station, a New Urbanist development outside of Portland, Oregon. It is much denser than a typical development, but because of its layout and relation to the region's light rail line, 22 percent of the residents take transit to work every day. Studies of vehicle miles traveled in the San Francisco Bay area show that suburban residents drive twice as much as residents in pre–World War II "Main Street" neighborhoods and four times as much as the urban core of San Francisco, where densities are fantastically high.

As for the argument that there is plenty of open land . . . the fact that most of the Nevada desert is wide open doesn't make me feel better, Mr. Cox. Most of us want open space in our own regions.

If Mr. Cox is so sure about the virtues of suburbia, let's let the two systems compete equally. Equal funding for transit and highways. Equally easy approval for New Urbanist projects and conventional subdivisions. Equal infrastructure investments in urban and suburban areas. I think he would be surprised at the results.

—*January 26, 2001*

Fair Growth First

At last, someone told us the emperor has no clothes! Common sense tells us we should not leapfrog infrastructure and lay waste to our open spaces just because we cannot make our urban centers into places people want to live. But somewhere along their way, the antisprawl leaders lost their way. The problem with the smart growth movement is that, armed with large grants, some of us are trying to impose a one-size-fits-all policy that threatens fragile rural communities and imposes a greater burden on the poor than the well-off. Perhaps it is time for a moratorium on smart growth until we can agree on a common definition.

—*February 2, 2001*

AUTHOR'S RESPONSE

Just a few comments in response to the comments on my op-ed on smart growth.

1. As regards the loss of agricultural land, the U.S. Department of Agriculture, under a Clinton-Gore administration, found that urbanization is no threat.

2. I reject outright the "antitransit" label. My proposals for transit, enunciated for more than a decade, would increase transit ridership but lower unit costs (thereby increasing service levels and lowering fares) and provide five times as much rapid transit for the available money (busways, etc.). Those who pursue policies

that limit transit ridership would be more appropriately labeled antitransit, regardless of the high offices they hold in the industry. What is good for transit as an industry or bureaucracy is not necessarily good for the riders and taxpayers, as the last thirty years should surely have taught us.

3. Smart growth policies, especially impact fees, have exacerbated the housing affordability crisis in California. Rationing home ownership by raising prices through impact fees removes the bottom rungs of the economic ladder.

4. Not only is Los Angeles not a sprawling urban area (by comparison with others around the nation), it is one of the densest urban areas in the country. Outside of New York, there is no larger area of high density.

5. Yes, denser cities have shorter trips but not enough shorter to negate the additional trips that occur from having more people in a square mile or kilometer. At the census tract level, traffic volumes tend to rise approximately 8 percent for each increase of 10 percent in density. That slows down traffic and increases air pollution.

6. The reality is that there have never been walkable cities of 5 million people, much less 10, 15, or 30 million.

7. I am intrigued by proposals to equalize subsidy levels for transit and highways. It would make sense if based on passenger miles. Of course, most of the expenditure on highways is user fees, not subsidies (just like payment to a city-owned electric utility is a user fee, not a subsidy). Right now, transit receives many, many times the subsidy per passenger mile as the street and highway system.

—February 18, 2001

AUTHOR'S UPDATE

It would be a mistake to characterize my views as favoring sprawl. There is much more at stake than urban planning and how our cities look. Urban planning is a means, not an end. The issue is affluence and the economy—the democratization of prosperity that has attended suburbanization and automobile use in North America, Western Europe, Japan and Australasia. At the same time, our cities have emerged as the cleanest in recorded history and are getting more environmentally friendly every day.

The land rationing policies have destroyed housing affordability by driving prices up relative to incomes by an unprecedented amount. This has occurred from Portland to San Diego, London, Vancouver, Sydney, and Perth. In these urban areas, prices have exploded to the degree that five to ten years or more of additional gross income are required to purchase and pay for the median priced house. At the same time, where a liberal land use regime remains, housing prices have changed little in relation to incomes. Today, the fastest growing large urban areas in the high-income world—Dallas-Fort Worth, Houston and Atlanta—have retained their historic housing affordability as have many other urban areas. Federal Reserve Bank research indicates that urban areas with stronger land use policies tend to experience less economic growth. The standard defense is to use "demand" side arguments as the reason for the artificial housing cost increases. The economic principle, however, is not the "law of demand." It is the "law of supply and demand." House prices have escalated in a few places because urban planning policies have seriously restricted the supply of land for development, while piling on substantial additional costs through fees, and unnecessarily complicated processes and delays.

Home ownership is an important contributor to improving affluence and reducing poverty. It must be extended, especially to the African-American and Hispanic communities, where the home ownership share is a full third below that of the white non-Hispanic share. Smart growth policies are likely to keep this from happening. Thus, I am strongly in favor of reducing poverty and maximizing the spread of affluence. I am happy to support whatever urban form advances that agenda. The issue is people and their lives, not cities and how they look. Unfortunate experience has shown that smart growth is a step backward in this regard.

PRESCRIPTION FOR URBAN SPRAWL: ADAPTING SMART GROWTH STRATEGIES TO A BIG CITY

Michael Woo

With the right policies and the political will to see them through, even Los Angeles could become a smart growth city.

The invention of the term *smart growth* by former Maryland Governor Parris Glendening was a masterful stroke of political phrase making. At a time when the high-tech sector of the economy was viewed positively as a driving force for progress and innovation, smart growth took its place alongside smart cars, smart cards, smart finance, smart homes, smart menus, smart kids, and other previously unexpected juxtapositions of smartness with things that were not considered inherently smart.

But what is so smart about smart growth? It constituted a rational alternative to mindless urban growth and mindless opposition to urban growth. It suggested that urban growth could be tolerated, and perhaps even desirable, if certain conditions were met. While there is no official scripture that defines smart growth, the basic tenets include the following:

- efficiency, not redundancy

- land use, transportation, and infrastructure policies coordinated to ensure that new urban development maximizes the efficient use of existing infrastructure, instead of wasting public expenditures on unnecessary new infrastructure

- compact development patterns instead of urban sprawl

- emphasis on transit, pedestrians, and bicycle transportation instead of dependency on private automobiles

• infill urban development instead of new growth on the periphery of urban areas requiring loss of open space and agricultural lands.

The problem with smart growth is not with its basic principles, many of which are a restatement of traditional urban planning principles that have been around for a long time. Instead, the fundamental question is whether smart growth is usable on a practical level. Can smart growth be used as an organizing principle to introduce systemic change into a system designed to resist external pressure for change?

Synonymous with urban sprawl, air pollution, and traffic gridlock, the City of Los Angeles could be a model urban laboratory for the application of smart growth practices. Compared to the small towns, suburbs, and larger cities with a history of local grassroots environmentalism that sustained the importing of smart growth ideas, Los Angeles is a more challenging test. If smart growth can take root in the hard, dry soil of Los Angeles, it will be a signal about the staying power of smart growth concepts.

Current trends in the Los Angeles real estate market point to a historic shift in the scale and form of urban development. After decades of efforts to expand the population of downtown residents, a real estate boom has produced thousands of new downtown apartments and condominiums, and some estimates project a doubling of the current downtown population of twenty-four thousand within ten years. The city's mayor, Antonio Villaraigosa, regularly talks about smart growth and transit-oriented development, and he appointed a new planning director and a number of city commissioners who share his vision of a "green city." In response, developers have proposed a wave of multistory, mixed-use buildings along some of the corridors of the expanding Metro rail system, a marked contrast with the stereotypes of single-family homes and low-rise commercial strips that used to characterize urban form in Los Angeles.

Yet, in order to reorient the city's growth patterns, it will be essential to move beyond the dominion of individual officials and discrete development projects to the broader realm of policy. In the face of significant evidence of changing market conditions and evolving consumer preferences, it is time to revise the current system—which worked so well for decades as the engine that produced the low-density, urban sprawl pattern of development which historically characterized Los Angeles—toward an urban model that supports smart growth objectives.

Reorienting the system may require months or even years of staff research, negotiation with stakeholders, and the public vetting that accompanies the process of lawmaking. But if planning policy can be shifted in the direction of smart growth, this vision of sustainable urban development can be realized— both in Los Angeles and elsewhere.

- *Promote successful examples of compact, near-transit, infill development that fit well with their surrounding neighborhood.* To throw the full weight of official support behind smart growth, development projects consistent with smart growth objectives should receive the highest priority in staff-time allocation and permit-expediting processes. This would send a clear message to developers and the general public about the seriousness of the city's intent to change development patterns.

- *Be mindful of the inherent conflict with the missions of other city departments.* Dedicated to improving the flow of auto traffic, a city's traffic engineers may fight for street widenings or other improvements that directly contradict pedestrian amenities or urban design features supported by smart growth policies. The same might hold true for public safety—for example, a fire department may ask for a site plan ensuring fire truck access that undermines the smart growth characteristics of a development project. Depending on the circumstances, smart growth advocates may need to resort to direct confrontation within the bureaucracy or seek political support from sympathetic elected officials to intervene in the dispute.

- *Be fearless about addressing the role of private automobile use in urban areas—a key issue.* The role of cars, and the need to provide space for their use when driven or parked, is central to the relationship between land use and transportation policies—which is at the heart of a smart growth policy agenda. If one adds up the cumulative amount of space dedicated for parking (including multistory parking structures) in Los Angeles's Central Business District (CBD) and lays out the spaces horizontally relative to the total amount of all space in the CBD, the ratio of parking to overall space would be 81 percent. (For comparison purposes, the same exercise in San Francisco would yield a ratio of 31 percent; in Manhattan, a ratio of 18 percent.)

- *Don't waste time trying to eliminate privately owned cars. Rather, limit their use to trips for which there are no alternatives to using a car.* Other cities, such as Tokyo and Curitiba, Brazil, have relatively high rates of personal car ownership but low rates of daily car use. In the Tokyo area, one of every two adults owns a car but 92 percent of daily commuters use rail to get to work. In Curitiba, one out of three adults owns a car but two-thirds of daily trips are by bus.

- *To change individual behavior, use a "carrot-and-stick" approach.* Practical smart growth policies will offer viable alternatives to private auto use as an incentive and will use inconvenience and added expense as disincentives to car use. Coordination with transit operators is essential to convince otherwise skeptical car owners that transit is a real alternative to their car use. This means particular attention to the need to expand the frequency of feeder buses and shuttles connecting transit stations to residential areas located beyond a half-mile radius.

- *Parking requirements are a key variable directly under the control of city government.* Off-street parking requirements should be severely reduced (or even eliminated) for development in areas well served by transit. Many developers will respond immediately to the prospect of saving $15,000 to $35,000 per parking space that they are not required to build. However, the developers' favorable reactions may be tempered by their apprehension about the reaction of lenders, who may condition their financing, or of lessees, who may condition their leases on the availability of parking because they believe that consumers will insist on access to parking. Consequently, changes in parking policy may require intensive outreach to developers, lenders, major commercial tenants, employers, labor unions, home owner and neighborhood associations, and other stakeholders.

- *Transportation demand management (TDM) goals need to be incorporated into every major project.* Developers and employers need to understand that they are the first line of defense in reducing the traffic impact of new development. Now may be the time for a new generation of tougher regional air quality standards driving more sustainable local land use and transportation policies, such as the recent decision of the air quality management district in California's Central Valley to assess fees on development projects that cause a disproportionate share of new long-distance commuting trips.

- *Send a clear, consistent, and early message about new planning priorities to all of the stakeholders.* The quasi-judicial role of a planning commission ruling on individual applications for development projects tends to lead to ad hoc, fragmented decision making. It is far better to start proposing smart growth–consistent changes at an early stage, from the project applicant's first contact with the planning department staff, or even earlier, when the developer is first conceptualizing the project. This means that the city's smart growth agenda needs to be converted into policy and clearly communicated at the earliest possible opportunity throughout the planning department's staff and to developers, architects, neighborhood groups, and other stakeholders, instead of waiting for projects to appear before a planning commission hearing. If the planning commission is taking the lead in promulgating smart growth policies, the process can begin with commission adoption of a resolution or policy statement declaring the smart growth concepts intended to guide future development decisions, and then disseminating the policies to stakeholders.

Urban sprawl wasn't built in a day, and the smart growth city will not blossom overnight. But with the right combination of visionary leadership, policy craftsmanship, skillful coalition building, adroit communication, and political will, even a city like Los Angeles could be transformed from the poster child of sprawl into a model of sustainable development.

MICHAEL WOO

was the first trained urban planner elected to serve on the Los Angeles City Council, on which he chaired the Transportation and Traffic Committee and was a member of the Planning and Land Use Management Committee. He currently serves as one of Mayor Antonio Villaraigosa's appointees to the Los Angeles City Planning Commission and is board chairman of Smart Growth America. Woo teaches urban planning at the University of Southern California and, at the University of California, Los Angeles, a special course on sustainable development in China.

HOW WE PAY FOR GROWTH

William Fulton |

California's Proposition 13—a citizen antitax initiative—has turned out to be the most important planning law in the state. Almost thirty years after its passage, author William Fulton discusses how Prop. 13 has altered the nation's attitude about how to pay for growth and, in the process, has been a major force in shaping the urban and suburban landscape we see throughout the country today.

Once upon a time, growth was good. This was not just because there was a philosophy that more people improved a community or a state but because there was a financial system based on the assumption that as communities grew, the value of their properties would grow commensurately. So paying for the cost of new growth by taxing everybody—or, at least, all the property owners—was considered fair, because in the end everybody would benefit.

All that went out the window almost thirty years ago—on Tuesday, June 6, 1978, when the voters of California passed Proposition 13 (Prop. 13), a citizen initiative that cut property taxes by more than half.

Prop. 13 is commonly credited with touching off a national tax revolt that has continued to this very day, as evidenced by the George W. Bush administration's 2003 $350 billion tax cut. But as my fellow writers at *California Planning & Development Report* and I pointed out in a report we published on the twenty-fifth anniversary of Proposition 13, in June 2003, Prop. 13 did much more than increase the pressure to cut taxes. It altered the nation's entire attitude about how to pay for growth—and, in the process, it has been a major force in shaping the urban and suburban landscape we see throughout the country today.

Very simply, the Prop. 13 psychology changed our view of growth from good to bad. New development that once helped us prosper now threatened to bankrupt us. As a result, the concept that "growth must pay for itself" became deeply embedded in our national psyche. And that has changed everything about the planning and development game.

Fiscal zoning and competition between municipalities for tax revenue is nothing new. Neither is the vigorous political jockeying within any community over who pays for new growth, nor the slow-growth desire to "pull up the drawbridge," nor even the practice of requiring two-thirds voter approval for local school bonds. All these things existed before 1978. But all were accelerated in California by the passage of Proposition 13.

Part of Prop. 13's intent, of course, was to reduce the size of government by reducing the amount of tax revenue available. But it is not the basic impulse of government to cut its own size. Rather than do that, local government agencies throughout the state have gone into survival mode in two different ways. First, they have intensified their competition with one another for the revenue sources available. Second, they have been endlessly inventive in finding new sources of revenue that are not subject to Prop. 13's limitations.

And because local government revenue sources are so closely tied to land and real estate development, this new "post–Prop. 13" culture was quickly translated into tangible changes on the urban landscape, many of which were tied to post– Proposition 13 revenue-raising strategies.

The "auto mall" is now common throughout the United States, but it was invented in California—not by the auto industry trying to sell cars but by local governments trying to capture sales taxes. The plethora of outlet malls, entertainment retail centers, and regional malls is also partly the result of Proposition 13. So is the boomlet in the creation of new cities in the last twenty years— because for the first time in history, a California community could incorporate by transferring money out of the county treasury rather than raising taxes. Many of California's sprawling regional development patterns are also the result of Proposition 13. Well-located cities have been able to cherry-pick retail centers, high-end housing, and other tax "winners." Meanwhile, starter homes and other tax "losers" have been relegated to distant locations on the metropolitan fringe, typically in unincorporated areas, where county leaders are desperate to generate any types of revenue they can get.

Similarly, California has become home to some of the most peculiar revenue-raising mechanisms in the history of American public finance. Parcel taxes, previously not permitted, are now common. Mello-Roos taxes were invented specifically to circumvent Proposition 13 and in the process created a municipal bonding mechanism that many on Wall Street still don't understand. Development impact fees are now a basic part of the California landscape—as is the "nexus consultant," whose job it is to prove the relationship between the fee being charged and the problem being created by the project. The state has also seen creative use of many different types of assessment districts. The end result has been to shift most of the cost of new infrastructure from payers of property tax to developers and new home buyers.

What is perhaps most surprising is that this basic model of California planning—the post–Prop. 13 model, we'll call it—has survived all the upheavals of the last three decades. Slow-growth sentiment has chilled whenever the real estate market has tanked, but it hasn't vanished. Even when there was nary a construction loan to be found in the whole state, land developers kept going after specific plans and development agreements, and slow-growthers kept suing them and putting their projects on the ballot.

Similarly, just when the fiscal zoning fad should have been fading into the background, the harsh financial realities of the 1990s gave it new life. In 1992 and 1993, the state government reminded the locals who is boss by shifting 25 percent of the property tax in the state—somewhere around $4 billion—away from cities and counties to the schools. Housing and other property tax–oriented development projects have been a bad deal ever since Proposition 13 passed. Now they're a much worse deal. And it's pretty clear that when the dust settles from the current state budget crisis, local governments will be more desperate than ever for new revenue—and will use land use authority more aggressively than ever to pursue that revenue.

In short, even in the twenty-first century, we seem to be operating with more or less the same planning and fiscal architecture that we've had for close to two decades—an architecture that has led to unnecessary competition among cities, ghettoizing of land uses, and regional imbalances in our large metropolitan areas.

As usual, a wide variety of incremental land use reforms are inching their way through the California legislature this year. But even if they pass, none will have a fraction of the impact of Proposition 13—a citizen antitax initiative that has turned out to be the most important planning law in California, and the bell-wether of the most important shift in the psychology of growth politics in the United States in the past thirty years.

WILLIAM FULTON

is president of Solimar Research Group and editor and publisher of *California Planning & Development Report,* author of *Guide to California Planning* (2nd ed., Baltimore, MD: Solano Press Books, 1999) and *The Reluctant Metropolis: The Politics of Urban Growth in Los Angeles* (Johns Hopkins University Press, 2001), and co-author with Peter Calthorpe of *The Regional City: Planning for the End of Sprawl* (Washington, D.C.: Island Press, 2001).

This article was originally published by Planetizen on June 2, 2003.

RESPONSES FROM READERS

Community Redevelopment Agencies Are Also to Blame

Speaking as someone who has a little experience with auto malls in California, I think Mr. Fulton has a point. However, there is another very strong local tax reason for auto malls that he didn't mention. The redevelopment powers of a local city's community redevelopment agency (CRA) can also be used to offer very attractive deals to car dealers, and there are few businesses whose needs match better with the powers of a CRA.

First, CRAs do have the power of eminent domain, so they can acquire land, in large chunks, in a way that no private landholder could. Second, CRAs can issue tax-exempt debt to finance the acquisition of the land and even the construction. Since the savings are passed through to the tenants, this is another major savings. Third, the new tenants can get ad valorem tax abatements. Fourth, the remaining property taxes now go to the CRA for a period of several years, taking the county's share.

Now, in California, a good share of the sales taxes goes back to the city where the sales were made, as general funds. This was Mr. Fulton's main point, and it is a strong one.

However, the overall structure of a CRA's power in parcel accumulation through eminent domain, tax-exempt borrowing for land acquisition and real estate improvements, ad valorem tax abatements for tenants, capture of the remaining ad valorem taxes for the CRA, and sales tax capture for the CRA's sponsoring city makes a very powerful package.

Like just about any other business, auto sales can be very competitive. When dealers are offered very attractive terms to relocate to a new city, almost all will listen very carefully. Some will accept the first offer, but others will shop around —which means, in many cases, going to the present host city and saying, "We've got an offer to move to City Y; why don't you have a CRA like they do?" Gee, guess what, now every city is throwing money at auto dealers with both hands just to attempt to stay even. *—June 4, 2003*

What about California Environmental Quality Act (CEQA)?

More than Proposition 13, I think that the California Environmental Quality Act (CEQA) was influential in shaping California's landscape during the last thirty years. No doubt, Prop. 13 dramatically changed a city's ability to pay for new growth, but CEQA, with its uncompromising standards, is the cause for sound walls enclosing subdivisions, high-speed six-lane divided arterials, and green-field, pod-oriented development. It would be interesting to have a study of growth in California under the hypothetical scenario of Prop. 13 without CEQA. I suspect that, based on economics and elimination of the CEQA voice, we'd see more compact growth than seen in the last thirty years. *—June 12, 2003*

WHAT IS THE NEW SUBURBANISM?

Joel Kotkin |

Joel Kotkin, author of a report on "New Suburbanism," introduces the new planning theory, clarifies what it means, and describes how it remains very much a work in progress.

Ever since The Planning Center published its original report "The New Suburbanism: A Realist's Guide to the American Future" in 2005 (Costa Mesa, CA), my colleagues and I have been asked repeatedly for a more precise definition of what we mean by the term *New Suburbanism*.

Put simply, New Suburbanism represents an effort to create better suburban communities. It is a philosophy of planning, design, and development that aims to improve all of the complex elements that make up a successful community—governmental, physical, economic, social, and environmental—creating a flexible template for a wide range of existing and newly designed suburbs.

One critical aspect of New Suburbanism lies in its pragmatism. One cannot always assume, for example, that building a new town center, constructing denser housing, or introducing mixed-use development will automatically improve quality of life—though these strategies can be useful, as we illustrated in our report. In some communities, physical infrastructure systems may be more important, such as schools, parks, and water systems.

New Suburbanism is not a new design paradigm that seeks to compete with or discredit principles of New Urbanism. Instead, our perspective represents a broad-based attempt to find the best, most practical ways to develop and redevelop suburban communities.

SUBURBAN INSPIRATION, OLD AND NEW

New Suburbanism embraces many of the principles championed by the smart growth and New Urbanism movements but finds most of its inspiration in already successful developments dating well before the development of New Urbanism.

These developments include The Woodlands, outside of Houston, Texas; Irvine, California; Columbia, Maryland; and Reston, Virginia.

These market-oriented developments have successfully incorporated a mix of uses and ethnicities while providing a well-balanced ratio of jobs and housing. They have also usually managed to preserve a significant amount of open space, feature neighborhood centers, steer away from strip commercial development, and integrate extensive bicycle and pedestrian paths.

In addition to an examination of relatively recent suburban development in the United States, an even longer historical perspective has also been critical to our viewpoint. Looking over the historical evolution of cities, particularly during the writing of my book *The City: A Global History* (New York: Modern Library. 2005), it became clear that suburbia grew not merely as a result of "white flight" or a conspiracy of oil companies, auto firms, developers, and governments. All may have played a role, but we believe suburban, multipolar places flourished mostly because they offered consumers something traditional cities all too often could not: safety, good schools, privacy, and space.

FLAWED ANTISUBURBAN ARGUMENTS

As a result, we do not approach suburbs with the disdain and contempt that unfortunately informs much contemporary thinking. Many students I run across now equate suburban development with monotonous, irresponsible sprawl. More extreme New Urbanists, such as James Howard Kunstler, regard suburban development as inherently wasteful and evil. Kunstler writes, hopefully, that due to rising energy prices, suburbs "are liable to dry up and blow away." "Let the Gloating Begin," he says, predicting that a general catastrophe will hit the suburbs, and urges people to leave these places as soon as possible (James Howard Kunstler, "Let the Gloating Begin", *Clusterfuck Nation*, November 8, 2004).

A less extreme but still flawed notion contends that metropolitan areas dominated by auto-centered suburbs somehow lack the intrinsic community values that informed traditional cities. Andrés Duany, for example, has written that in sprawling, multipolar cities like Phoenix and Houston "civic life has almost ceased to exist" and that many people in these areas complain about their quality of life. (Andrés Duany, Elizabeth Plater-Zyberk, and Jeff Sperk, *Suburban Nation: The Rise of Sprawl and the Decline of the American Dream*, New York: North Point Press, 2000, 95, 137).

Yet one would be hard-pressed to say that a Phoenix or a Houston has a less vibrant civic culture—witness the remarkable grassroots response of Houston to the Katrina disaster. Nor can one say that there has been more widespread disenchantment there than in more traditional transit-oriented cities, such as Boston, Chicago, and San Francisco. After all, these cities have been losing population and jobs while the sprawling ones have been growing. Places like Houston and Phoenix are also developing many of the elements of civic culture, such as great hospitals, museums, and cultural centers, that tend to arise in vibrant, commercially vital cities.

SUBURBS ARE THE FUTURE

Rather than reject such cities, we are committed to their improvement. All of our analysis of current and likely future trends reveals that sprawling multipolar cities with overwhelmingly auto-dependent suburbs will continue to enjoy economic and demographic growth over the next several decades.

Specifically, we looked at where jobs are being created. Fortunately, my work for the annual *Inc. Magazine* "Best Places" survey with economist Michael Shires has given me access to the most recent data. Overwhelmingly, the fastest job growth—including in such fields as information and professional business services—has taken place in suburban areas around older cities or in the famously sprawled out multipolar cities of the West and the Sunbelt, including Boise, Ft. Myers, Las Vegas, and Reno.

We believe developers and planners must look at what consumers are communicating through their migration patterns. Although a strong market niche exists for traditional urban living, surveys and census data reveal that this niche remains relatively small, perhaps no more than 10 to 20 percent of the total population. Surveys conducted in California, a heavily urbanized state, show that most people—upward of 80 percent—want single-family homes.

Now some will say, "Yes, but if you asked them if they wanted a single-family home that is two hours away from their job, or a condominium loft only 15 minutes away, they would choose the loft." Yet this may be a false choice. As jobs move to the suburban periphery, the commutes for residents there, as Harvard's Ed Glaeser has demonstrated, (Edward L. Glaeser and Matthew E.Kahn, "Sprawl and Urban Growth," Harvard Institute of Economic Research, May 2003, 5) tend to be shorter than the commutes of those who live in denser, more transit-oriented places. Far-flung Houstonians, for example, suffer somewhat shorter average commutes on average than New Yorkers or Chicagoans.

For these reasons, it seems a bit quixotic to push for a future that takes its signals from the dense, centralized, transit-dependent urban past. We instead should follow a pragmatic, market-oriented approach to improving the areas in which people increasingly choose to live. For example, in a low-density suburban community that seeks to retain its single-family character, it may be more appropriate to introduce small-lot, single-family detached housing rather than assume that multifamily apartments and lofts must be part of the solution.

Yet, for all the growth and evident market appeal of suburban areas, we do agree with critics that many suburbs clearly need to improve, particularly in terms of their public spaces and treatment of the environment. Most important, however, we also know from past experience that better suburbs are possible.

In the short run, we New Suburbanists seek to learn how to make the increasingly decentralized metropolis work better. Looking to the future, we envision a heavily wired "archipelago of villages," with relatively compact and economically self-sufficient communities spread across our landscape. The time has come to acknowledge the dispersed reality of our metropolitan future and to find out how to make it a better one.

JOEL KOTKIN

is an Irvine Senior Fellow with the New America Foundation. He is also the author of *The City: A Global History* (New York: Modern Library, 2005). He is currently writing a book on the American Future for Penguin Books.

This article was originally published by Planetizen on April 24, 2004.

RESPONSES FROM READERS

What Is the New Suburbanism?

How intriguing that Kotkin would cite Reston, Virginia, and Columbia, Maryland —a master planned and a greenbelt city, respectively—as inspirations for the "New Suburbanism." The only problem with this theoretical framework is that modern suburbs resist master planning, mixed-use zoning, multifamily housing, and open space planning—all of which were essential elements in the success of both Columbia and Reston.

In fact, it is American suburbs' market orientation that is essential to understanding their development—now and in the future. One could argue that both Phoenix and Houston are largely agglomerations of suburban edge cities since neither metropolis has a definable city center. While Kotkin defends edge cities' hegemony in job creation, he fails to cite what makes suburbia attractive to soccer moms and CEOs alike—free and easy transportation networks, corporate office parks, and cul-de-sac housing on quarter-acre lots.

Of course, all of this is made possible by gobbling up cheap farmland, or in the infamous phraseology of America's number one home builder, Toll Brothers, "chasing ground." As Kotkin and his New Suburbanism acolytes attempt to address the misuse of open land and scarce natural resources, market forces will continue to withstand any attempt to shape the great American frontier.

Are better suburbs possible? Certainly, but the market forces that were unleashed more than a half century ago to create the modern American suburban landscape, much of what I term *faceless sprawl,* are unlikely to succumb to better design or planning   —*July 18, 2006*

Americans Prefer the Suburbs

Fact is, most Americans with kids (like me) love suburbia. If we can afford to get away from crime, crowds, pollution, and poor schools, we're outta there. Why try to design planning systems that deny us that choice?

As a kid in the 1970s, I grew up in an older, more urban neighborhood, and seriously, I was at times stressed out by the problems of violence, theft, and intimidation at school and in the neighborhood. There were racial tensions and economic tensions that we'd all wish Americans could overcome, but they exist. I couldn't have been happier when my family moved to a small ranch just outside a suburban community right before I entered high school. I felt much safer, enjoyed school, learned more, and developed into a better human being because my parents cared enough to find a more supportive environment for their kids.

I feel the same way today, and I think you'll find that most of us suburbanites are there for the schools, the peace, the space, the beauty, the quiet, and the friendly (or at least nonviolent!) neighborhood relations. I commute to a downtown job, and the long drive is annoying, but what's annoying compared to the peace I have knowing my kids are safe at school and at home all day?   —*May 1, 2006*

Long Drives and Peace Knowing the Kids Are Safe

Do you also get that feeling of peace knowing that your long drive to work is causing the global warming that will leave your kids a less livable world when they grow up?

New Urbanists have designed many streetcar suburbs, such as Orenco Station in Oregon, which have all the benefits of the auto-oriented suburbs that you live in but that support walking and transit use rather than making people totally auto dependent.

If you lived in one of those new streetcar suburbs, you could say, "The long transit ride to work is annoying, but what's annoying compared to the peace I have knowing that my kids are safe at home all day and that my kids will have a decent world to live in when they grow up rather than facing energy shortages and climate chaos."

—*May 2, 2006*

PRESERVING THE AMERICAN DREAM BY COST, NOT COERCION

Randal O'Toole |

Freedom of choice in housing, transportation, and lifestyle should be controlled by monetary costs, not inefficient and coercive land use policies.

Is the American dream compatible with smart growth? That depends, of course, on how you define the terms *American dream* and *smart growth*. During the Preserving the American Dream conference in February 2003, we defined *American dream* as "mobility and affordable homeownership," and we defined *smart growth* as "coercive land-use planning aimed at compact cities, often combined with expensive and ineffective rail transit."

The conference was held in Washington, D.C., and featured Andrés Duany, Wendell Cox, Peter Gordon, and many other speakers. About a third of the speakers discussed flaws in the smart growth platform, a third presented our "American dream" alternative, and a third talked about how they have defeated smart growth and promoted the American dream in their communities.

Some of the people at the conference were libertarians who would oppose government coercion in any form. But most were not, and if smart growth worked, far fewer people would have attended the conference. Many at the conference might support smart growth if it kept its promise to reduce congestion, provide affordable housing, and otherwise promote urban livability.

In fact, as defined above, smart growth is incompatible with the American dream because smart growth leads to more traffic congestion and less affordable housing. Urban growth boundaries, impact fees, and land use regulations drive up the cost of housing. All else being equal, compact cities are more congested than low-density ones because the reductions in per capita driving that accompany density never match the increases in density. Compact cities can relieve congestion by building lots of highways, but rail transit exacerbates congestion because it diverts funds from highway improvements that do far more to keep people mobile. Smart growth fails in other ways, too, leading to more air pollution, higher urban-service costs, and less urban open space.

If you are planner, you may believe that we need to "redefine the American dream." But that is not your choice. More than 80 percent of all travel in the United States is by automobile, and more than 80 percent of Americans say their ideal home is a single-family, detached house with a yard. Americans have made those choices for good reasons.

Home ownership helps Americans build wealth, partly because most business start-ups are partially funded on second mortgages. Automobiles have done even more to make Americans wealthy by giving people access to better jobs, lower-cost consumer goods, better housing, and other things they can't reach by transit or on foot. Policies that increase congestion and housing costs make America poorer, and they fall the hardest on those Americans who are already poor.

No one will object if you can convince some Americans to have a different dream. Andrés Duany distinguishes between New Urbanism, which he defines as voluntary, and smart growth, which he considers coercive, and he told the conference that he is willing to let his New Urbanist developments withstand a market test. Many, if not all, of his developments have passed that test, including Kentlands, which we toured, and where (we were told) home values are greater than similar homes on larger lots in more conventional suburban developments nearby.

No one at the conference objected to Kentlands or other New Urbanist developments that meet market demand. Personally, I wouldn't mind living in a place like Kentlands; I just don't think cities have the right to force people to do so by prescriptive zoning or artificially high housing prices.

Our goal is to preserve the American dream by giving people freedom of choice in housing, transportation, and other lifestyle issues while making sure that they pay the full cost of their choices.

- We support highway tolls that vary by the amount of congestion.

- Where air pollution is a problem, we support pollution emission fees that would encourage people to keep their cars clean or to retrofit their cars with pollution-control devices.

- We support cost-effective transit and subsidies to transit-dependent people in the form of transit vouchers, rather than subsidies to transit bureaucracies.

- We support devolving zoning power to individual neighborhoods, so that neighborhoods can control their own destiny instead of being under the smart growth planning sword of "infill" and "neighborhood redevelopment."

No doubt some will respond to this commentary by fretting over paved-over farmlands, the military costs of safeguarding oil in the Middle East, and the General Motors conspiracy to destroy America's transit systems. You can find responses to these and many other smart growth myths on the American Dream Coalition website (http://www.americandreamcoalition.org) and in my book *The Vanishing Automobile and Other Urban Myths* (Bandon, OR: Thoreau Institute, 2001).

If your goal is to help your constituents and other Americans achieve their dreams and aspirations, then we will be glad to work with you to find ways to reach that goal. If, however, your goal is to impose your utopian ideal of an auto-free, high-density lifestyle on others who may not share that ideal, then I look forward to helping any of your constituents who choose to oppose you.

RANDAL O'TOOLE,

an economist with the Thoreau Institute, organized the "Preserving the American Dream" conference held in Washington, D.C., in February 2003. An Oregon native, he has lived most of his life in Portland but currently lives in Bandon, Oregon.

This article was originally published by Planetizen on March 17, 2003.

RESPONSES FROM READERS

O'Toole Misses the Point Entirely

O'Toole wants to give people "freedom of choice . . . while making sure that they pay the full cost of their choices." Sounds good to me. The World Resource Institute estimates that—not counting the cost of pollution—we subsidize petroleum roughly $300 billion annually. This includes everything from the depletion allowance (a write-off for oil producers) to petroleum-related health costs (like accidents) to roads to our once-a-decade military adventures in the Middle East.

The military costs are absolutely necessary, incidentally, since we stopped producing enough petroleum domestically more than thirty years ago. Even the

Alaska National Wildlife Refuge won't reverse this trend. With this subsidy, in effect we're paying people a few bucks a gallon to buy gas for their cars and charging them to ride transit.

O'Toole is right about congestion but ignores the other advantages of compact development. No more than ten minutes of walking daily significantly reduces late-life health problems. Should we start charging sprawl for chronic health problems stemming from inactivity?

The trouble with Libertarian arguments is that they ignore the heart of the matter. We have sprawl now not because someone chose it but because a series of tiny, regulatory steps made sprawl the path of least resistance—an unintended consequence. —*March 17, 2003*

We Need a New Definition of Smart Growth

As one who is involved mostly as a civic activist in the transportation end of things—fighting for much-needed highways and opposing multibillion-dollar fixed-rail boondoggles that do nothing to alleviate congestion—I have found "smart growth" to be nothing more than a weapon to beat people like me over the head with, as if building new roads is wrong but spending billions on light rail that few use is somehow "smart."

I've seen people who live on three- and five-acre lots and drive SUVs opposing new highways because "we need to stop sprawl." I've seen people who live in my former sprawl-pattern neighborhood in North Bethesda [Maryland] oppose a conference center and other density near a Metro station. These people use "smart growth" as a shield for their NIMBYism and selfishness.

I've seen former Maryland Governor Parris Glendening tell the world that Kentlands and Annapolis are models of smart growth because of "excellent design," though neither is accessible by transit and Kentlands is twenty miles outside the urban core of D.C.

I am seeing politicians in Maryland touting Clarskburg, a neo-urbanist village being built maybe fifteen miles north of Kentlands, as smart growth, just because it has compact design and could be facilitated by a light rail system that will take an hour or more to get to any jobs. Why is putting forty thousand people so far from jobs in D.C. or Bethesda, Maryland, "smart"?

I've seen people in ultra-liberal, Portland-like Takoma Park fight plans by Maryland and our local transit authority, WMATA, to build townhouses at the Takoma Metro station because it would take away their park.

In my view, smart growth is a weapon—nothing more—to be used by NIMBYs opposed to anything near them (such as highways, which the smart growthers see as incompatible), or to make areas more unaffordable (such as Arlington, Virginia, and Bethesda, Maryland).

In my view, what smart growth should be about is investing in decaying and older cities and suburbs. It should be about putting housing and jobs and retail in areas with existing infrastructure—not packing forty thousand people out in the middle of a cow pasture like Clarksburg.

Smart growth should not be incompatible with highway building. Smart growth should not be about using coercive government policies such as artificial urban growth boundaries, which do not work and only push population farther out.

Until anti-highway NIMBYs, wealthy landowners who don't want "newcomers" near them or affordable housing, or politicians like Glendening who want to blame sprawl and developers for the world's problems so they don't have to make tough decisions on new infrastructure can agree on a universal, market-based definition of smart growth, I believe this is nothing more than a fiction, a pipe dream, and another smoke screen to con voters and taxpayers into thinking their local government is doing something when in fact, they are not.

—*March 18, 2003*

ZONING IN A TIME WARP: THE COMING "OVERSUPPLY" OF SINGLE-FAMILY HOMES

Harriet Tregoning

Ozzie and Harriet zoning won't work for twenty-first-century house-holds and preferences. Without reforms, many communities could be headed for a crisis in household and community wealth.

The history of growth and development in the United States is a complex interaction among private investment and enterprise, government-funded infrastructure investment, tax incentives, government-backed home mortgages, and, yes, zoning. Arthur C. Nelson, a professor of urban planning at Virginia Tech, notes in a recent article that from 1954 through 1980, a federal planning grant program for local government zoning was based on a Federal Housing Administration model clearly biased toward single-family, owner-occupied, detached housing units and against multifamily and attached housing ("The Longer View: Planning Leadership in the New Era,"*Journal of the American Planning Association,* Fall 2006). The same federally promoted planning program also promoted the rigorous separation of land uses. This planning model was based on serving a population that consisted primarily of two-parent households with children—the stereotypical Ozzie and Harriet household as noted by Kenneth L. Jackson in his book *The Crabgrass Frontier: The Suburbanization of the United States* (New York: Oxford University Press, 1985).

However, the demographics and realities of the twenty-first century are very different from those of, say, 1967. Not only are households getting smaller, but they are also getting older. The proportion of the population over age 65 is projected to increase from 12.4 percent in 2000 to 19.6 percent in 2030—or from 35 million in 2000 to an estimated 71 million in 2030. According to the U.S. Census Bureau, the number of persons age 80 or older is expected to increase from 9.3 million in 2000 to 19.5 million in 2030 ("Midyear Population, by Age and Sex," table 094, international database, http://www.census.gov/population /www/projections/natdet-D1A.html.)

A SNAPSHOT OF A CHANGING UNITED STATES

	1967	2006	2025
U.S. Population	200 million	300 million	349 million
Average Household Size	3.3 persons	2.6 persons	2.5 persons
Households with Children	46%	32%	28%
Households without Children	54%	68%	72%
Single-Person Households	16%	26.5%	28%
Vehicle Registrations[1]	98.9 million	237.2 million	Not estimated

Source: U.S. Census Bureau, *U.S. Interim Population Projects.* Washington, D.C.: U.S. Department of Commerce, March 2004.
[1] "Trend Lines: The 300 Million Mark," *The Washington Post,* October 17, 2006.

Baby boomers will live longer than any previous generation as empty nesters. And they do not want to get old like their parents did—they want to delay the inevitable as long as possible by pursuing healthy lifestyles, living in vibrant, walkable communities, and enjoying all of the cultural and mental stimulation they can.

But are we building those communities? In most communities across the country, the Ozzie and Harriet zoning that exists, much of it dating back to before 1970, still enormously favors the continued building of large-lot, single-family homes on greenfield parcels far from the center of cities and towns. Professor Nelson's own analysis of the nation's occupied housing concluded that more than 50 percent of our housing stock is in large-lot, single-family housing, with 21 percent in single-family housing on small lots and 25 percent in attached units.

Building new homes on small lots or building townhouses, apartment buildings, or condos is often much more difficult to do, if not actually prohibited by current local zoning. A trend in recent years has been to increase the minimum lot size in an effort to ensure that the property value will be sufficiently high to cover government service costs and possibly exclude households with lower means from the community.

Yet, according to Professor Nelson, of the nearly 32 million new households we will see by 2025, only 12 percent will have children. A whopping 88 percent will be households without children, with nearly a third of the total growth attributed to single-person households. Overall, the percentage of households *without* school-age children at home will rise to 72 percent by 2025, from 54 percent in 1967.

Will these households want to buy the large suburban house of the aging baby boomer who would like to move into a renovated loft condo in the city? We appear to be heading for a probable mismatch in housing type, relative to the coming demand for housing. In some communities, we are already there.

Housing Bubble or Market Mismatch?

Many home buyers are familiar with the concept of "driving 'til you qualify." It is not unusual for buyers to suffer a sixty-mile (or more) one-way commute in metropolitan areas where housing prices are high. Since they spend so much time in their car, they typically opt for luxury, spaciousness, and horsepower—usually at the expense of fuel economy. According to the U.S. Environmental Protection Agency, the average 2006 model vehicle achieves a paltry twenty-one miles per gallon, while many of the sport utility vehicles favored by the long-haul commuters get less than half that. However, the specter of rising energy prices and high heating, cooling, and transportation costs is making the house with a long commute less attractive.

Analysts are busy observing the effect of rising energy prices, higher financing expenses, and the impact of a six-month inventory of unsold new homes, many of them at the outer edges of metropolitan areas. New housing starts are down significantly, while the price of existing homes fell 2.2 percent in September 2006, the largest monthly decline recorded in the nearly forty years the number has been tracked, according to the National Association of Realtors ("Existing Home Sales," October 25, 2006, http://www.realtor.org/Research.nsf/files/EHSreport.pdf/$FILE/EHSreport.pdf). Clearly, some home owners are feeling the pinch.

Unfortunately, it is not clear who the purchasers for their homes will be now or, even more questionably, in the future. Yet we continue to deliberately channel the entrepreneurialism and enterprise of our important building and construction sector into what looks like obsolete (or at least oversupplied) housing types. Much of the concern about a housing bubble seems to focus broadly on metropolitan areas; certainly, a large drop-off in new housing construction in large exurban developments will have repercussions throughout the regional economy. However, there seems to be little discussion of the role of a market mismatch in the incipient housing bubbles looming over many regions.

Iceberg Lettuce: Another Reason to Reform Zoning

So the answer is obvious but not easy: reforms are needed—zoning reforms that allow new development to be more responsive to current and future market demand. A national survey in 2004 by the National Association of Realtors found 86 percent of respondents preferring development in existing communities, not in the countryside, and 50 percent favoring transit over new roads, which won only 18 percent support. The *Minneapolis Star Tribune* reported that prospective buyers of new homes in the next few years, by a margin of 61 to 39 percent, lean toward mixed-use, pedestrian-friendly, transit-oriented neighborhoods certain to reduce their car dependency ("Strong Market Preference Is Driving Industry toward Smart Growth," editorial, November 2, 2004.)

But in the thirty thousand units of local government across the country that have zoning authority, most regulations that deal with zoning, building codes, street widths, and subdivisions either do not permit or severely constrain the more compact, mixed-use development that prospective home buyers are increasingly demanding. Even where such development is allowed, the approval process typically requires much more time—more public meetings, more back-and-forth with regulatory agencies—before a developer can build these new types of products. The old adage "time is money" is never more true than in the building industry, so a tortuous path to build a housing product that might be a better fit for the demand is unlikely to be chosen if the regulatory process makes conventional development shorter, quicker, easier, and more familiar.

This should not be a concern just to some home builders or to a few far-flung home owners. When antiquated zoning encourages home builders to respond to demand for new housing by building more single-family homes, the resulting oversupply could negatively affect the value of every similar home in that market.

Such a decline would have significant financial impacts on the household wealth of many Americans. According to Dean Baker at the Center for Economic and Policy Research, the percentage of U.S. household wealth that is represented by equity in an owner-occupied home is up to 48.5 percent from 38.7 percent a decade ago, and home owners are increasingly considering the equity in their houses as a replacement for savings ("The Housing Bubble Fact Sheet Issue Brief," Washington, D.C., July 2005). In addition, the housing sector is an enormously important part of the national economy. New housing starts are a bellwether of economic health. By itself, housing construction represents about 5 percent of the gross domestic product. Clearly, a significant decline in housing value would have significant repercussions for individual home owners and would send ripples through both regional economies and the national economy.

Some might ask, "Why would builders continue to build suburban, single-family homes if the demand for them fell?" In part, it is the long lead time necessary for a builder to bring a housing product to market; the market might change, but the builder is committed. In part, it is the structure of the industry; big builders represent around 20 percent of the industry, but their large-scale projects create 80 percent of the housing that gets built—it is tough for them to suddenly begin to build closer in to the center of a region on small infill lots (although many large builders are creating new infill divisions). But, in part, it is also a forecast of consumer preferences that looks in the rearview mirror. Remember twenty-five years ago when you went into the produce section of the supermarket? All you saw was iceberg lettuce—crisp, mild, long keeping. The supermarkets must have thought, "Wow, Americans *love* iceberg lettuce. Look at how much they buy!" Growers must have thought, "It's incredible how much supermarkets and consumers adore this iceberg lettuce. Let's plant more!"

Of course, the reality is that many consumers desired other types of lettuce but had little choice in the matter. Today, you walk into a grocery store and encounter dozens of lettuce types in the produce section—endive, green leaf, red leaf, romaine, mesclun, mache, arugula, even prewashed, prepackaged, crouton-included, ready-to-eat salads, currently a $2.7 billion market. We still sell and produce a lot of iceberg lettuce (although the market share is declining, two-thirds of all the lettuce grown in the United States is still iceberg), but we now enjoy many other choices.

In most housing markets, for years the vast majority of new construction has been single-family homes. As soon as some other choices are more widely offered—in their region or others—these homes may well be oversupplied while their market share shrinks.

Zoning reform is no easy task. At a minimum, it requires a broad constituency supporting, if not demanding, those reforms. Smart growth groups, transit advocates, affordable housing proponents, and environmental organizations are natural allies, but given the potential impacts, a much broader set of actors could be engaged. Business leaders, civic associations, and chambers of commerce are obvious choices. Even home owners, who traditionally have resisted zoning reform in an attempt to protect property values, should be able to get behind these reforms once they understand the market dynamics—the potential threat to their nest eggs.

The large and small implications of our nation's changing demographics are becoming more clear. It is also becoming clear that communities that do not address the disparity between what their regulations allow and what the coming market demands risk jeopardizing the prosperity and economic stability of their region and potentially of the nation.

HARRIET TREGONING

is director of the Office of Planning for the District of Columbia. Prior to this she was the Director of the Governors' Institute on Community Design and executive director of the Smart Growth Leadership Institute (a project of the national non-profit advocacy organization Smart Growth America). She is the former secretary of planning and former secretary for smart growth for Maryland. While at the United States Environmental Protection Agency, she founded the National Smart Growth Network, a national partnership program designed to inform and accelerate innovative smart growth policies and practices.

TRANSPORTATION

Introduction by the Editors of Planetizen

Transportation is a fundamental component of urban planning. The efficient movement of people and goods is a basic requirement for a livable city, and cities with poor or inadequate transportation infrastructure rarely are able to achieve a high level of success. Roads and highways, railways (including subways, metros, and elevated and trolley lines), sidewalks, waterways, and airports are all part of the infrastructure critical to the functioning of a city.

Despite the importance of transportation, one could be forgiven the impression that it is the forgotten stepchild of urban planning. The design and construction of streets and sidewalks simply doesn't have the same cachet or appeal as other aspects of planning, such as historic preservation and commercial revitalization. Oftentimes, transportation planning actually gets done by civil engineers. Though these engineers are well schooled in the nuts and bolts of transportation planning, they are required first and foremost to make sure that roadways adhere to government standards, and they often lack the interest or know-how to design infrastructure in a way that creates good urban spaces.

The result is increasingly recognized as a general lack of sensibility in our transportation system. Our roads and highways are designed to move cars, but they offer little to no consideration of the people inside those cars. Even many public transit systems display a blatant disregard of their users—sometimes dropping them in less than hospitable places with hundreds of yards to walk before reaching any real destination.

Most planners can agree on the primary goal of transportation planning: make it easy to move around the city. How best to go about achieving that apparently simple goal is where much of the dispute lies.

With the growing interest in smart growth, many planners and communities are interested in encouraging alternative modes of transportation to the automobile. The use of public transit of all types—buses, light rail, subways, monorails, streetcars—has experienced a resurgence in recent years. And the walkability of our cities' streets has once again become a consideration among transportation planners.

However, public transit has many critics. Its opponents argue that the sprawling American landscape is unfit for efficient transit service and that Americans' propensity for living in low-density suburban communities gives little hope for change. Rather than continue to invest in expensive transit infrastructure projects that will serve only a small fraction of the population, some feel that cities should focus on managing the ever increasing number of cars on the road.

Although many communities still aspire to build their way out of traffic jams, and while road-widening projects tend to be popular, there is a growing understanding that traffic congestion cannot be solved by simply building more roads. Congestion pricing—the idea of charging for access to road space according to the level of demand—has emerged as a popular strategy for managing the demand for highways. The success of central London's experiment with a congestion charge has given the concept a major boost. More and more communities are contemplating installing high-occupancy toll (HOT) lanes—dubbed "Lexus lanes" by their opponents because of a perceived or real threat of economic discrimination.

But no matter where one's view rests on the transportation ideology spectrum, one notion that enjoys universal agreement is the desire to bring transportation planning back into the fold by tightly linking it with land use and development decisions. When development and transportation infrastructure are planned in a coordinated fashion, traffic congestion can be managed more effectively and the costs of new roads or transit can be captured. This thinking can be seen in the increasingly popular concept of transit-oriented development, which involves building around existing transit stops, such as Orenco Station in Portland, Oregon.

Planning experts are also reaching consensus on the need to more accurately price parking. While the notion of "free" parking is widespread, urban economists are quick to point out there is, in fact, no such thing. The cost of land, construction, and maintenance can sometimes add up to tens of thousands of dollars per parking space. By passing on the actual costs of parking to the driving public, people are more likely consider alternatives, thereby decreasing the number of cars on the road and lowering congestion.

Some transportation experts, anticipating an era in which cars no longer rule, are devising plans to transform city streets from auto-only zones into multimodal and multiuse spaces. Instead of cars, streets could be dedicated to bicycles or used as park space.

As of yet, to the chagrin of some and to the relief of others, the day when cars no longer reign supreme over the American landscape appears far off. But whether the strategy taken is to create more walkable, transit-friendly, and bike-friendly communities that draw drivers out of their cars or to manage car use more efficiently through marketplace signals, the ultimate test will remain whether we can get from point A to point B with the least amount of fuss.

TEN KEYS TO WALKABLE COMMUNITIES

Dan Burden |

Walkable communities are celebrated destinations that create a sense of place and promote economic development. Dan Burden identifies the top ten strategies planners can use to craft a walkable community.

The following ten items are key indicators or measures taken to achieve prosperous, walkable, healthy, livable communities. No towns or village centers in the United States today exhibit all of these measures in whole, comprehensive, or complete ways. Rather, the good towns are organic (springing from the fertile soil of local creativity and sensibility), and they are progressing toward true walkability and livability. These towns have crystal clear visions for the future, and they are in the process of achieving each of these measures. Many towns with one or two of these keys are moving forward to succeed with most or all of the other measures.

These walkable communities may not be seen as good places for cars, but they are very livable and worth finding. These towns are talked about, celebrated, and loved for their uniqueness and ability to champion the natural environment and human spirit.

1. *Compact, lively town center* (or many compact villages, in larger towns or cities). Buildings frame streets; block lengths are short. Merchants take pride in their shops' appearances. Great varieties of stores offer local products and services. Significant housing is found at downtown or village center sites. The place has a unique and distinct personality or character.

2. *Many linkages to neighborhoods* (including walkways, trails, and roadways). People have choices of many routes from their homes to the center and most other locations. The most direct paths are walking routes. All sidewalks are five feet wide or wider, and many are buffered from streets by planting strips, bike lanes, or on-street parking. Well-maintained sidewalks are found on both sides of

State Street, Santa Barbasa, California | Photo by Dan Burden

most arterial and collector roadways. Sidewalks are cleared during winter months, if necessary. Most neighborhood streets have sidewalks on both sides. Bike lanes are found on most principal streets. Streets with higher volume or speeds almost always have bike lanes. Most streets are barrier free with ADA (Americans with Disabilities Act) ramp access to and from each block in all directions.

3. *Low-speed streets* (in downtown and neighborhoods, 20 to 25 miles per hour is common). Motorists are given adequate speed design controls so that most behave well in the downtown or village center and near schools, waterfronts, historic neighborhoods, parks, and other public areas, yielding to pedestrians. Motorists make their turns at low speed. Few places force motorists to stop. Yield conditions are most common.

4. *Neighborhood schools and parks.* Most children are able to walk or bicycle to school and small nearby parks. There is limited or no busing of school children, and at least 40 percent of all school trips are by foot or bicycle. Most residents live within half a mile (preferably a quarter mile) of small parks or other well-maintained and attractive public spaces.

5. *Public places that invite children, teenagers, older adults, and people with disabilities.* Many services and facility designs support and attract many children, teens, senior citizens, and people with disabilities to most public spaces. Public

restrooms, drinking fountains, and sitting places are common in many parts of town, especially downtown.

6. *Convenient, safe, and easy street crossings*. Downtowns and village centers have frequent, convenient, well-designed street crossings. Pedestrians using commercial areas rarely have to walk more than 150 feet from their direct lines of travel to reach crossings. People crossing at intersections, whether signalized or not, rarely wait more than thirty seconds to start their crossings.

7. *Inspiring and well-maintained public streets*. Streets are attractive, balanced, and colorful; feature sidewalks, planter strips, and medians (when appropriate); and handle a diversity of needs. Many streets feature on-street parking, and larger-volume streets have bike lanes. Homes and buildings are brought forward, relating to the street. There is little or no off-street parking. Sidewalks are centered and surrounded with attractive edges, a planter strip to the street side, and an edge or attractive transition to the private property.

8. *Mutually beneficial land use and transportation*. People understand and are given reason to support compact development, urban infill, integral placement of mixed-use buildings, and mixed-income neighborhoods. The built environment is of human scale, with attributes that invite positive interaction and complement the surrounding neighborhoods. Heritage buildings and places are respected. People understand that small, local stores help create community as well as convenience. Residents desire and find ways to include affordable homes in most neighborhoods. Transit connects centers of attraction with schedules so frequent that times need not be posted. All residents feel they have a choice of travel modes to most destinations. Most people live within walking distance— half a mile (with the majority within a quarter mile)—of 40 percent of the services and products they need daily or weekly, including small grocery, pharmacy, hardware, bank, "doc-in-a-box" medical, day care, dry-cleaning, post office, and other essential services.

9. *Celebrated public space and public life*. Streets, plazas, parks, and waterfronts are fun, festive, secure, convenient, efficient, comfortable, and welcoming places. Suitable places exist to host parades or public speeches, and people feel encouraged to take part in community parades, festivals, outdoor concerts, and other public events. Public space is tidy, well kept, respected, and loved. Many of these favorite places are surrounded by residential properties, with many "eyes-on-the-streets" to add security and ownership of these spaces. These areas have

many places to sit. Few or no buildings have large blank walls, and few or no open parking lots exist off street. Any existing parking lots have great edges and greens. The natural beauty and quality of the community environment are not only appreciated but celebrated, with annual awards given to the best developers, neighborhood parks, buildings, retailers, and private placement of new park benches. Barbershop quartets, brass bands, string quartets, small dance troupes, local theater groups, and other opportunities for community participation are alive and well. People can find public places for practice, fun, and spontaneous play.

10. The community has many "green" streets, with trees and landscaping. The town form respects the need for plenty of green and open space. Heritage trees line many streets. Development practices call for street trees and planter strips; homes are clustered to maximize green space. Trails and passageways through natural areas are featured in many parts of town. Landscaping is respectful of place, commonly featuring native species, drought-resistant plants, colorful materials, stone treatments, or other local treats. In desert and high-country areas, many methods are used to minimize use of water and other precious resources.

11. *Many people walking.* Many diverse people are walking in most areas of town. The community has no rules against loitering. Lingering in downtowns, village centers, schools, city hall, civic centers, waterfronts, and other public places is encouraged and celebrated. Street musicians and entertainers are welcomed. Children rarely need to ask parents for transportation, especially to school, parks, and downtown.

DAN BURDEN

is a nationally recognized authority on bicycle and pedestrian facilities and programs. He has had twenty-seven years of experience in developing, promoting, and evaluating alternative transportation facilities, traffic-calming practices, and sustainable community design. He served for sixteen years as the Florida Department of Transportation's state bicycle and pedestrian coordinator, and he currently is executive director of Walkable Communities Inc., a nonprofit corporation helping North America develop walkable communities, and a partner with Glatting Jackson.

This article was originally published by Planetizen on June 25, 2001.

THE PRICE OF PARKING ON GREAT STREETS

Donald C. Shoup |

Practical policies can mean big benefits for the streets on which they are enacted. With performance-based parking prices, local revenue return, and parking increment finance, everybody wins. This chapter was adapted from a speech delivered at the Urban Land Institute's Great Streets Symposium in Washington, D.C., January 17–20, 2006.

How can curb parking contribute to a great street? To help create great streets, a city should (1) charge performance-based prices for curb parking and (2) return the revenue to the metered districts to pay for added public services. With these two policies, curb parking will help to create great streets, improve transportation, and increase the economic vitality of cities.

Performance-Based Parking Prices

Performance-based prices will balance the varying demand for parking with the fixed supply of spaces. We can call this balance between demand and supply the "Goldilocks principle" of parking prices: the price is too high if many spaces are vacant, and too low if no spaces are vacant. When a few vacant spaces are available everywhere, the prices are just right. If prices are adjusted to yield one or two vacant spaces in every block (about 85 percent occupancy), everyone will see that curb parking is readily available. In addition, no one can say that performance-based parking prices will drive customers away if most curb spaces are occupied all the time.

Prices that produce an occupancy rate of about 85 percent can be called "performance-based" for three reasons. First, curb parking will perform efficiently. Most spaces will be occupied, but drivers will always be able to find a vacant space. Second, the transportation system will perform efficiently. Cruising for curb parking will not congest traffic, waste fuel, and pollute the air. Third, the economy will perform efficiently. The price of parking will be higher when demand is higher, and this higher price will encourage rapid parking turnover. Drivers will park, buy something, and leave quickly so that other drivers can use the spaces. For parking, transportation, and economic efficiency, cities should set prices to yield about an 85 percent occupancy rate.

Local Revenue Return

Performance-based prices for curb parking can yield ample public revenue. If the city returns this revenue to pay for added public spending on the metered streets, residents and local merchants will support the performance-based prices. The added funds can pay to clean and maintain the sidewalks, plant trees, improve lighting, bury overhead utility wires, remove graffiti, and provide other public improvements.

Put yourself in the shoes of a merchant in an older business district where curb parking is free and customers complain about a parking shortage. Suppose the city installs meters and charges prices that produce a few vacancies. Everyone who wants to shop in the district can park quickly, and the meter money is spent to clean the sidewalks and provide security. These added public services make the business district a place where people want to be, rather than merely a place where anyone can park free if they can find a space. Returning the meter revenue generated by the district to the district for its own use can convince merchants and property owners to support the idea of performance-based prices for curb parking.

Suppose also that curb parking remains underpriced in other business districts. Everyone complains about the shortage of parking in these districts, and cars searching for curb parking congest traffic. No meter revenue is available to clean the sidewalks and provide other amenities. In which district would you want to have a business?

Performance-based prices will improve curb parking by creating a few vacancies, the added meter revenue will pay to improve public services, and these added public services will create political support for performance-based prices.

Parking Increment Finance

Most cities put their parking meter revenue into the city's general fund. How can a city return performance-based meter revenue to business districts without shortchanging the general fund? The city can return only the subsequent increment in meter revenue—the amount above and beyond the existing meter revenue—that arises after the city begins to charge performance-based prices. We can call this arrangement *parking increment finance*.

Garages tucked under apartments line a San Francisco street. | Photo by Donald Shoup

Parking increment finance closely resembles tax increment finance, a popular way to pay for public investment in districts in need of revitalization. Local redevelopment agencies receive the increment in property tax revenue that results from the increased property values in the redevelopment districts. Similarly, business districts can receive the increment in parking meter revenue that results from performance-based parking prices. More meters, higher rates, and longer hours of operation will provide money to pay for added public services. These added public services will promote business activity in the district, and the increased demand for parking will further increase meter revenue.

Citation Revenue Sharing

If curb parking is priced to make spaces available, the meters must be enforced. To increase local support for enforcement, the city can share with neighborhoods the revenue from parking citations. Citation revenue can, for example, pay to repair and maintain the sidewalks on metered streets. Instead of opposing enforcement, merchants and residents will see illegally parked cars as citation

Surface parking lots along Venice Boulevard in Los Angeles. | Photo by Donald Shoup

opportunities and will begin to support enforcement. The city will manage parking more effectively, and the neighborhood will receive more revenue to make its streets clean and safe.

By extension, the city can share the revenue from red-light cameras with neighborhoods. Because the city wants to reduce vehicle accidents and increase pedestrian safety, it can offer to install red-light cameras at appropriate inter- sections and spend the citation revenue to repair and maintain the nearby sidewalks. The cameras will encourage motorists to drive more carefully, and the few who do run red lights will pay to improve pedestrian safety. Except for those who run red lights, everyone will win.

Pilot Program

Cities can use a pilot program to test Goldilocks parking prices for curb parking, combined with local return of the meter revenue. Any business district that wants a pilot program can request it. Because dirty and unsafe streets will never be great, the added parking meter revenue can initially pay for clean-and-safe programs. Many communities may value clean and safe streets more highly than free but overcrowded curb parking. Parking may not be free, but it will be convenient and worth paying for.

DONALD C. SHOUP, FAICP,

is professor of urban planning at the University of California, Los Angeles and has written many books and papers on parking, including *The High Cost of Free Parking* (Chicago, IL: Planners Press, 2005), a Planetizen Top Book for 2005, which explains the theory and practice of parking management.

This article was originally published by Planetizen on March 29, 2006.

THE PRICING REVOLUTION
ON THE ROADS

Peter Samuel

We can't build our way out of traffic congestion, but we can use road pricing to provide some options and can make some money while we're at it.

The Texas Transportation Institute calculates that traffic congestion costs Americans $70 billion a year. This is our analog of the empty shelves and long lines of Soviet-era supermarkets—the result of dysfunctional government monopolies of road service not pricing a scarce commodity properly. Like Soviet bureaucrats, the state departments of transportation and metropolitan planning organizations are preoccupied with long-range construction plans, constantly revising what is supposed to result twenty-five years out (in addition to routine house-keeping—filling cracks, fixing dents in guardrails, removing trash, and so forth). However the revolution in road pricing provides us with a new opportunity to refashion the way we provide road service—and if not to do away with congestion completely, at least to offer options to get past the congestion on urgent trips and to mitigate what's left.

California's Route 91 Express Lanes were the first example of using price to manage traffic flow. They work by charging sliding toll rates. As of October 2006, the rates vary from between $1.15 and $8.50 in hourly slots, with different price schedules each day and the current price posted on signs at the entry point. The 91 Express Lanes pricing schedules are amended every six months, or whenever needed, to keep the prices at a level to attract enough traffic but not so much as to threaten a breakdown of the flow.

More sophisticated still is the dynamic pricing in use to manage HOT (high-occupancy toll) lanes on Interstate 15 in San Diego and on Interstate 394 west of Minneapolis. In these lanes, equipment embedded in the pavement uses electro-magnetic induction to read the metallic mass of vehicles passing over, generating

The 91 Express Lanes in Riverside, California. | Photo courtesy of Orange County Transportation Authority

constant measurements of lane occupancy. The changing density of traffic is used with algorithms of motorists' responsiveness to price ("price elasticity of demand" is the economists' jargon) to generate real-time appropriate prices that can change as frequently as every few minutes. A constant auction is, in effect, being conducted, allocating scarce road space to motorists who value it most highly and keeping out those who value the road space less at the time and whose presence in the roadway would only risk causing the flow to break down.

California's 91 Express Lanes are commonly pictured in PowerPoint presentations at the Transportation Research Board and at planning conferences with traffic all jammed up in the free lanes on the right while to the left of a line of yellow plastic lane dividers are a few sparsely separated vehicles tooling along freely at 70 miles per hour. The pictures evoke different reactions. One is a supposed "equity" issue, a notion that there is something unseemly about people being able to buy their way past congestion.

But where's the equity in treating unlike trips all the same? Some trips are far more urgent than others—journeys to make an air flight or to meet an appointment, for example, are higher-value trips than sightseeing or shopping trips. In the first type of trip, speed and reliability of trip time are very valuable to people.

In the second type of trip, time and reliability really don't matter much. Only a silly kind of superegalitarianism that wants everyone to suffer equally can object to giving people the right to buy superior service on the roads, a right they have in every other sphere of life. It is true that, although all income groups make some use of toll express lanes, the rich will make greater use of them. They make greater use of Federal Express versus the U.S. Postal Service, of first class versus coach on airlines, of hired help versus do-it-yourself choices, of better housing and finer food versus the alternatives, and so forth. A superegalitarian approach to the roads—denying those with an urgent trip the opportunity to buy a fast ride—ends up punishing most those with a high value of time saved today. Most users of toll express lanes—as on California Route 91, where tolls are as high as 80 cents per mile but average 30 cents per mile—are selective in using them and more often than not use the free lanes. In other words they use them only when their value of time saved is greater than the toll, not because of their member-ship in any particular income class.

But on their face, those presentation pictures of relatively empty express toll lanes seem to be showing inefficiency. Isn't there a lot of pavement being wasted? viewers wonder. Actually, no. Even as measured by the simple vehicle throughput per lane per hour rate, the express lanes are significantly more efficient than the clogged lanes. Exact measurements vary, but most show more than 1,500 vehicles per lane per hour in the toll express lanes versus barely 1,000 in the free lanes in peak hours.

It is well established by traffic observations that as an expressway lane becomes heavily loaded, throughput becomes increasingly unstable. Seemingly random events trigger a motorist to brake and the perturbations travel back; soon the flow has broken down, and stop-and-go, creep-and-crawl driving conditions pre-vail over much of the roadway. Average speeds, which have been edging down, collapse precipitously. Because vehicles can travel closer together at lower speeds, throughput doesn't drop as much as speed, but it drops significantly all the same—by perhaps a third. Just at the point where motorists need maximum capacity, they lose a slab of it.

No precedent for such pricing existed when it was first introduced a decade ago. Yet in all cases so far, the various pieces have been made to work well from the beginning. And contrary to the predictions of traditionalists in the toll industry, the public accepts the varying prices.

We can't just build our way out of congestion as long as we continue to offer scarce and expensive urban peak hour service for nothing. There is no way we can fund the extra capacity to satisfy the demand that free roads generate. We clearly can't plan our way out of congestion either; nor can we "transit" or "bike" our way out of congestion. We've been trying all that for several decades now and spending vast resources in the attempts.

We can, however, price our way out of congestion and actually make some money, as is proven every day where it has been tried—on the Route 91 Express Lanes in California, and the HOT lanes in San Diego and Minnesota. There will be a need for some new building, some new planning, and some new transit (rubber-tired), but the key to tackling congestion and making roadways more efficient is letting the market work by pricing road space.

PETER SAMUEL

is editor of *TOLLROADSnews* (www.tollroadsnews.com) and a senior fellow in transportation studies at Reason Foundation in Los Angeles, CA. He has taught economics and written for newspapers and magazines on various public policy issues. In the past twelve years, he has specialized in writing about tollroads and road pricing. Of British and Australian extraction, he has been in the Washington, D.C., metro area for the past twenty-four years.

A CELEBRATION OF INDEPENDENCE: HOW TEMPORAL USE OF STREETS CAN BE A CATALYST FOR CHANGE

Kenneth E. Kruckemeyer

Many cities have announced their intent to reduce their carbon fuel dependency and abide by the Kyoto Accords, yet most are finding implementation elusive. Kenneth E. Kruckemeyer, a transportation strategist and Research Affiliate at the Massachusetts Institute of Technology's Center for Transportation and Logistics, imagines a kaleidoscope of temporal uses of our public streets, parkways, and open spaces that will jump-start a succession of incremental changes, bringing inexpensive but effective shifts in transportation and energy use.

Every Sunday morning, a million cyclists take to the car-free streets of Bogotá, Colombia, for fun, exercise, and socializing. It is reported that more than 2 million citizens (perhaps a quarter of the city's population) take part in this weekly *ciclovia*. Even those who do not participate in the spectacular, environmentally friendly activity benefit from reduced pollution and less noise as they talk to neighbors or play ball on streets that, for seven hours every week, are calmed by the absence of cars.

How we live, play, shop, and work today is the result of changes that have taken place over the past one hundred years of automobilization. It is reasonable to expect that weaning ourselves from car dependence may take just as long. These changes, however, need not be expensive, and they can have impressive immediate rewards, as the Bogotá example illustrates.

Even if we can imagine an energy-independent future, even if we understand this imperative, we seem to have little idea as to how to get there. Mayors of many cities have been quick to embrace the Kyoto Accord goals of reducing carbon emissions and slowing global warming, but many seem paralyzed to implement the steps necessary to achieve them. On the whole, both individual citizens and our political leaders seem unable to resist the urge to build our way out of traffic congestion, and our visions of better public transport are most often capital intensive and take years to implement.

Temporal changes in the use of our public rights-of-way, such as *ciclovia*, applied in incrementally more comprehensive patterns may be a key to successfully reducing carbon emissions and meeting environmental goals that otherwise seem to elude both the developed and developing worlds.

Temporal Use: Traditional and Contemporary Examples

The world is filled with examples of temporal changes in the use of public space; some, like weekly markets in a town square, go back hundreds if not thousands of years. Many streets had their moments when the parade went by, when the carts took produce to market, and when dogs slept in the middle of the road. This loss of "the commons" to the automobile has occurred over the past one hundred years in the United States, and has much more recently transformed public life in many developing countries. There is little respite on any street today because we are schooled to believe that streets belong to cars. Only a few take up street philosopher David Engwicht's advice and move the dinner table into the street to get the cars to slow down.

However, in some places the trend is being reversed through thoughtful innovations of use varying with time that are worth a look. Several Dutch cities with narrow streets in their town centers use signals to limit incoming traffic at the ring road to no more than can proceed through the center without congestion. Buses, arriving on a queue-jumper lane, proceed and return from the center of town on a good schedule. New York City, although not yet prepared to eliminate traffic entirely from the roadways of Central Park, continues to increase vehicular restrictions and yield more time to joggers and cyclists. A fishing village near San Sebastian in the Basque country, with only one street, restricts vehicular entry to one minute out of every ten; the rest of the time, the street belongs to pedestrians. In Auckland, New Zealand, curbside midday and nighttime parking becomes a combination bike and bus lane in rush hours.

These temporal changes differ from physical changes that delineate use (changing the proportion of a street designated for autos, pedestrians, and cyclists). Such changes—as in Copenhagen, where on-street parking spaces have been eliminated at the rate of 2 percent per year for the past thirty-five years to make space for expanded bike lanes and pedestrian precincts—are essential as well. As the ways of satisfying our mobility demands become more complex, we will need many strategies to accommodate them. We will need to figure out where bicycles with electric boosters, wheelchairs, Segways, walking school buses, and golf carts fit into the mobility spectrum. Hans Mondermann (of the Friesland Regional Organization for Traffic Safety) and Shared Space in England and Europe have successfully eliminated the traditional traffic engineering devices of signals, signs, curbs, and pavement markings at intersections and have substituted an "undifferentiated playing field" that makes all users more cautious, more respectful, and, ultimately, more safe.

Imagining the Future

It is temporal change that can be implemented most quickly—at low cost, under sponsorship of a neighborhood group or a government agency, and without an environmental impact statement. Temporal changes can be revised in either direction, as the benefits and mistakes become apparent. These changes can be part of a consistent progression of environmentally and socially integrative actions that will remake our physical and public world in the future as completely as it has been altered by the automobile in the past.

As an example, consider the roads of the Metropolitan Park System in Boston laid out by Frederick Law Olmsted for "pleasure vehicles [carriages and bicycles] only" in the late 1800s. Many of these park roadways have been transformed over one hundred years into access-controlled arteries, heavily used for auto commuting. Today, temporal relief from vehicular traffic occurs on a short section by Harvard University on Sunday afternoons and along the Charles River Basin on the Fourth of July.

Imagine the following progression of the return of these roadways to their original purpose, while at the same time helping move the metropolitan area toward fossil fuel independence. What if, starting this year, following the Bogotá example, bicycles, skateboards, and wheelchairs replaced autos for half a day every Sunday. Think about how these celebrations would transform the image of the city: the city's major parks and reservations, its zoos and arboretum, would all be easily accessible from every neighborhood and without parking problems. Think of families getting fresh air without the gas, time, and cost of getting to a weekend retreat; an elderly housing group out for exercise on stable adult tricycles; an excursion of teens meeting other teens from a different neighborhood. And think of people who live across the roadway from a park or esplanade who can now get there safely. In five years this celebration might apply to most of the five hundred lane-miles of parkway all weekend. Over the next period, perhaps twenty years, as public transport becomes more necessary and more successful at delivering high-quality, competitive service, the traffic lanes may be needed only during commuting hours and may consist of a mix of cars and low-impact buses. In a subsequent phase—perhaps in many years to come—rush-hour use of the roadways might be exclusively for public transport vehicles.

Then apply the ideas of temporal use and celebration to other city streets through a progression of changes. Some streets could be used for public transport in the rush hours, some for bicycle priority, others for school access. There would be more places for outdoor dining, for kids to play, and wheelchairs to roll. People would get exercise safely at lunchtime and buy locally at expanded farmers' markets. The transportation networks, noise and air pollution, energy consumption —the very image of the city—would change.

Implementation through Incremental Change

Turning streets over to nonmotorized use may be intoxicating! Celebrations are an awakening, but not the final state. If it can happen for a few hours in a day, one might imagine life where streets belong to everyone—not just those with enough money and skill to drive a car. The benefits of "street closings" flow to more than the immediate participants: the schoolchildren walking to school, the cyclists on errands, the elderly on scooters out to meet friends. They flow as well to the residents and businesses. Pollution goes down; personal safety goes up. The police officer passing by on a bicycle is more effective than a squad car racing by.

But where do all of the cars go? It is useful to remember that, per minute, one bus can carry as many people as three solid lanes of traffic! A folding bike can get you to the bus or train and at the other end speed you on to your destination. As has been learned in the residential *woonerf* of Holland or the walking streets of Copenhagen, cars for access and trucks for delivery are still permitted but they navigate slowly, in a supporting rather than dominant role.

And where does the money come from? Public coffers seem continually insufficient to pay the costs of road construction, maintenance, and traffic cops, as well as build and operate public transportation. But also consider the private expenditures. The annual cost of owning and operating a car in 2005, before the recent skyrocketing price of gas, was $7,800 (parking and tolls not included). Thus, for a metropolitan area of 2 million people, nearly $6 billion is being spent each year on getting around by car. (There are twenty-two "cities" larger than this in the United States, and fifty cities with more than 1 million.) Is it so hard to imagine that many of these people might choose to spend some of that money on transit if it worked really well for them (by not being bogged down in traffic, for example)? And I suspect that they would be very willing to spend the remainder on better housing, food, education, or even a nice vacation.

The Future Realized

Celebrations in the street that change accepted use are not an end to themselves, although they will be energized by contemporary concern over obesity and high gas prices. Temporal changes give people the option to imagine a different world, a different way to get around, a different view of the city by offering the chance to experience it. The choice is no longer limited to the car or by foot but stretches among many options—Segways, scooters, bicycles, tricycles, skates, skateboards, wheelchairs, tandems, pedicabs—for mobility, for fun, for exercise, for social interaction. The long-term benefits will come from changing the way we think about our public rights-of-way, the transportation systems that use them, and what it is like to live and work next to them.

KENNETH E. KRUCKEMEYER

is a transportation strategist in Boston, and can be reached via the Internet at kek@mit.edu.

MAKING TODS WORK: LESSONS FROM PORTLAND'S ORENCO STATION

Michael Mehaffy

A project manager gives a real-world account of the successes and failures of one of the nation's most closely watched new transit-oriented communities, and its role in the regional growth management strategy.

The planning practices of few jurisdictions are as closely studied—or as hotly debated—as those of Portland, Oregon. The region's innovative growth management system and transit-oriented development (TOD) efforts are hailed by some as near-perfect national models for livable growth and are bashed by others as clumsy infringements of property rights and free enterprise, reflecting only the unworkable utopian dreams of planners.

A growing body of evidence suggests the truth may lie somewhere between these extremes. Some things are indeed working in Portland and ought to be studied as models—or at least as clues for how to make things work better elsewhere. Other things are not working and ought to serve as cautionary tales.

A key strategy of the Portland regional approach has been to rezone land adjacent to light rail stations to create new mixed-use, transit-oriented development. In several prominent cases, the station areas have been designated as mixed-use town centers, following the New Urbanist program of well-connected, pedestrian-friendly streets and a diverse mix of housing, retail, and civic uses.

Orenco Station has emerged as perhaps the most prominent laboratory in that regional experiment, in part because it offers a real-world test of many specific aspects of that program. In Orenco Station, there is a pedestrian axis to the light rail station, around which a grid of alley-loaded "skinny streets" extends; a walkable town center of mixed-use shops, services, and residential; "liner" buildings with limited on-street parking and lots tucked behind; a range of housing types and prices, originally priced from $79,000 to over $500,000, as well as rental units; pedestrian-friendly street design and scale; "granny flats"

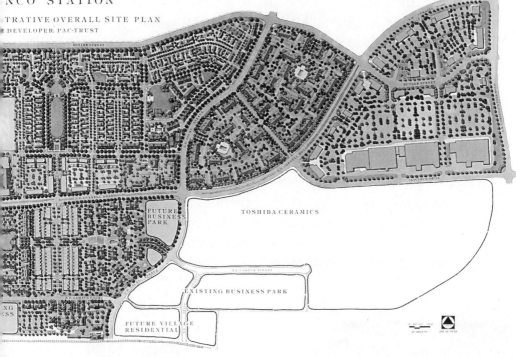

Master plan of Orenco Station. | Image courtesy of Orenco Station, LLC

and live/work units; loft units above retail; and, of course, much higher density (up to twenty-five units to the acre) than is typical for the American suburbs.

Skeptics suggested that PacTrust—the pension fund partnership and master developer for whom I served as project manager—was unwise to cooperate in creating this kind of development. After all, there were no real precedents even for attached product in that suburban market, let alone for the kinds of radical densities and other features proposed. But while the company was certainly wary of the dangers, research also suggested an unmet appetite in the market for this kind of community, one that has since been borne out.

In addition, a number of steps were taken to mitigate risk, including early sale of some parcels to codevelopers. Most significant, the company made it a condition that it would be given the flexibility to follow the market and protect its interests as needed; with that important limitation, it would commit to implementing the regional policy goals. This meant the company would become a full participant in writing the new zoning and working out the vision of the community, based on extensive market research, study of precedents, private-sector expertise, and entrepreneurial vision.

This relationship of trust and pragmatic collaboration with public entities was perhaps the most critical element in the decision to move ahead and to pursue all the ambitious features that were later realized. It may also have been the most critical element in the ultimate success of the project, as it set the stage for the detailed problem solving with jurisdiction staff that is critical in such a complex project.

In spite of the early skepticism, the community has been strongly embraced by the market. Initial sales and subsequent appreciation have been strong. The town center has attracted a strong mix of neighborhood retail and commercial services, including a grocery store, household goods, laundry, salon, dentist, restaurants, and other neighborhood-scale businesses.

Orenco Station Town Center. | Photo by Michael Mehaffy

In fact, our team was taken aback at the strength of the market response; going in, we did not regard the project as a major profit center, and we expected (and did encounter) the significant start-up diseconomies that are typical for such a pioneering project. We made no secret of our views—this was, after all, a regional laboratory kind of project. Team colleague Dick Loffelmacher stated unequivocally to the press: "The project is successful." Though PacTrust has largely remained focused on its profitable core business of industrial and commercial development, a number of its partners, consultants, and participants (including this author) have gone on to enjoy similar success on other, similar projects (Podobnik. 2002. "New Urbanism and the Generation of Social Capital: Evidence from Orenco Station," *National Civic Review,* 91(3), 245-255).

Moreover, a sociology study (Podobnik, 2002) has shown very high levels of resident satisfaction with the community, very high "social cohesion," and relatively high transit and alternate mode transportation habits (a 22 percent modal split versus about 6 percent regionally). Many of those automobile trips are also "captured" within the community, reducing overall travel. Considering the suburban setting, this achievement should not be underestimated.

But it is important to note that many features of the plan deviated substantially from planners' original prescriptive intentions. Most significant, the automobile —still the choice of most suburbanites for most trips—has been realistically accommodated, though in ways that better mitigate its negative effects on livability. Assuming automobile use declines with the rise of fuel costs and concerns about the environment and health, alternative modes are now much more viable.

Other aspects of the community show room for improvement. The feeling of "naturalness" of the place could be stronger, in part because of its disconnected suburban location and in part because of top-down design and production methods to achieve economies of scale and control. While the community does have an unusually broad range of product and price points, both economic and ethnic diversity could have been broader, and there was limited provision for more affordable homes. This has been exacerbated by rapid appreciation of home values in the community, even greater than typical appreciation elsewhere during this period.

In hindsight, the live/work townhomes, although successful enough to prompt a second phase, were not as successful as they could have been, in part because the workspaces were too small to be effective and because the split-level design complicated access for disabled users. Lower production costs and price points—more feasible in a more refined second-stage project—would have allowed even higher absorption and margins.

Perhaps most important, the team did not have control—or, in one notable case, sold off control—of key parcels of land surrounding the station. It was also an unhappy fact of history that the station location was on the periphery and removed from the major arterial roadway that bisects the site, in order to site the town center in a viable location. In a more ideal world, the team would have had better control over these conditions—and would have maintained that control.

In spite of these "lessons learned," however, the community has clearly achieved remarkable relative success on all these scores, and today it is a thriving, highly desirable neighborhood in the Portland area. It continues to serve as a laboratory offering important and useful lessons about how to make TODs work.

- *Density demands design*. Abstract land use designations are only the beginning. The essential task is to create a coherent neighborhood structure with livable features and services.

- *Build a great team*. Assemble a skilled, talented consultant team early on, led by private entities with vision and risk management skills, to closely collaborate and problem solve together.

- *Bring the jurisdictions and the private entities onto the same team*. Major challenges are still posed by obsolete national building codes, traffic engineering practices, and local zoning. Their solution requires the close cooperation and collaboration of public entities—from elected representatives down to desk staff—as well as skilled private consultants.

- *Do your homework*. The devil will be in the details of the design. Start with good market science, not only in assessing what buyers have already bought but in understanding potential buyers and envisioning what they will want and need. Then be prepared for lots of detailed problem solving and research.

- *Learn from history*. There are many valuable lessons in successful older neighborhoods and how their mix of uses functions successfully. Do not slavishly copy, but do not ignore the great problem-solving resources collected in traditional design.

- *Keep a firm hand at the tiller*. Do not let disparate owners or builders destroy the standard of design quality. Do not surrender control prematurely.

- *But let the design evolve.* At the same time, be prepared to allow many inputs and many hands, and let the design evolve with changing real-world conditions, while preserving a coherent neighborhood structure.

Perhaps the central lesson of Orenco Station—to be further established with ongoing research—is that there is indeed great potential for such transit-oriented and mixed-use development to create more livable, more sustainable neighborhood development. At the same time, formidable challenges remain.

For example, significant initial diseconomies in the complexities of mixed-use construction and management still exist. Closely related is an expensive requirement for very high quality customized design, beyond the narrow formulas of architectural or consumer fashion. Perhaps most onerously, there remains a massive burden of obsolete codes and regulations, and reform is badly needed. Similarly, the entitlement process is typically still far too complex, inefficient, and burdensome.

But if government needs to get its act together, private property interests need to do likewise. An equally formidable challenge is the continuing political attack on almost any form of community land use planning, motivated in part by a remarkably absolutist antigovernment debate. A closely related ideological cousin is the attack on appropriations of public infrastructure funding needed for light rail itself, and for the more coherent kind of development around it— often even when this funding is structured in innovative, accountable ways.

But in our view, such public actions come under the entirely proper constitutional mandate to promote the general welfare. In that sense, the freedom of consumers to choose to live in such communities—as they clearly do—is matched by the freedom of voters to choose the kind of public realm they will create in a democracy.

MICHAEL MEHAFFY

is a project manager, urban designer, and educator as well as president of Structura Naturalis Inc., an urban design and consulting firm based in Portland, Oregon.

This article was originally published by Planetizen on June 14, 2003.

URBAN DESIGN
Introduction by the Editors of Planetizen

Urban design is, simply put, the art of making "places." Residing at the intersection of architecture and planning, urban design involves the coordination of both macro- and micro-scale details to create desirable, functional, and attractive environments in which people can live, work, and play. From building orientation and street layout to the design of street furniture and lamp posts, good urban design is responsible for both the function and "feel" of a city.

When most people talk about urban design, they instinctively think about the public realm—the spaces between buildings made up by streets, plazas, and parks. These venues have traditionally been where good urban design can be observed by the public. Tragically, as Americans have moved out to the suburbs and started spending more time in their cars and backyards, the creation of quality urban spaces has been largely neglected. Local government, which was traditionally responsible for providing parks and other civic venues, instead focused its attention on encouraging (or discouraging) private development through a myriad of planning regulations and programs.

Today, many urban designers agree that the public realm is in crisis, and a growing number of citizens and professionals are calling for a greater emphasis on the elements of good urban design and public space. The primary focus of this work has been to reorient urban spaces away from cars and toward people. Commonly recognized elements of people-oriented design, including narrow streets, tucked-away parking lots, street trees, and street furniture, are some of the most popular ways that cities are retrofitting their public spaces.

A major force in the practice of urban design has been the New Urbanism movement. Founded by a group of architects interested in the comprehensive reform of urban planning and development, the movement emphasizes the creation of compact, walkable neighborhoods built on a gridded street system with a mix of uses and housing types. Also known as *neotraditional planning*, the New Urbanist movement advocates for a return to self-sufficient, walkable communities designed to encourage social interaction. These goals, many of which are shared with those of the smart growth movement, are achieved through observing a transect of rural-to-urban development, which stipulates what type of buildings should go into the varying districts of a city.

New Urbanism has been a polarizing force in the field of urban design. The movement's developments have been largely built on outlying green space and claim few successful infill projects, leading to the analysis that New Urbanism is simply a more compact form of sprawl. In addition, controversy has erupted over the movement's propensity to use classical or traditional vernacular architectural styles in its developments. Although not a true characteristic of New Urbanism (the movement's charter specifies only that new architecture must fit into its surroundings), several famous New Urbanist projects, such as Seaside, Florida, strongly dictate architectural elements, and the revival of the "front porch" has become widely recognized as the movement's signature trait.

Confusion over the impact of the form and function of design versus its style has led some to criticize the movement for creating communities that simply try to recapture the nostalgia of "days long gone" while actually doing little to address the real challenges facing urban areas. Indeed, many supposedly New Urbanist communities have turned out to be nothing more than pretty façades on typical suburban tract homes—a wolf in sheep's clothing. In response to the absence of criteria to approve or rate developments as official New Urbanist developments, the Congress for the New Urbanism (CNU) is working on creating a rating system of new projects. The CNU has partnered with the U.S. Green Building Council (USGBC), which has been very successful in creating a rating system for "green," or environmentally sustainable, buildings.

The green building field itself is another major force in urban design, with membership in USGBC growing tenfold between 2000 and 2006. Whether called "sustainable architecture" or "eco-friendly design," this new way of using design and materials to build new structures and reuse old ones promises to help reduce the ecological damage that buildings have on the landscape and the global environment.

All of these trends are positive signs for the health and well-being of urban areas. As greater focus is again placed on good urban design and the quality of the public realm, the vibrant civic life so sought after by many cities can once again become commonplace.

PLANNING FOR THE PUBLIC REALM

Alexander Garvin |

After more than half a century of focusing on the regulation of private property, planners and the governments they work for must return to their intended and essential role as the developers of a mixed-use and multifunctional public realm.

When one thinks of any city, one thinks of the public realm—the streets and sidewalks, the parks and plazas, the transit stations and stores. It is the fabric that knits the city and around which the city grows. The parks of Paris, the canals of Venice, the streets of New York—these are all the public realm.

The public realm provides the framework for private investment. Historically, governments have recognized that actions in the public realm can help shape development. To stimulate new development, cities plat and pave streets, install sewers, plant trees, and develop new parks. Central Park was originally built far north of the city to lure development up Manhattan Island. The boulevards and parks that Baron Haussmann built in Paris (in concert with new aqueducts and sewers) were a massive investment in the public realm, and they made Paris the premier city in the world.

Yet for the past fifty years, governments throughout the United States have been slowly abandoning this essential role. Since World War II, planning has shifted from strategic government investment in public works to government regulation of private property and private development. The results have been appalling: interminable and expensive approval processes, a growing property rights backlash, and a shoddy public realm.

Meanwhile, the public realm we have has become increasingly balkanized into single-function uses—streets for traffic, wetlands for plants and animals, storm ponds for runoff, playgrounds for children. Nothing is viewed in a context beyond that one function, and secondary effects are rarely considered—for example, that widening a road may increase traffic capacity but may also eliminate sidewalk space and decrease business for adjacent stores.

It is time to resurrect the practice of strategic government investment in creating a mixed-use, multifunction public realm. Though planners speak a great deal about mixed-use neighborhoods, they are typically referring to private property, such as apartments, offices, and shops. Yet the public realm can and should accommodate many uses. A street, for example, can accommodate cars, delivery trucks, transit, and bicycles. A sidewalk can accommodate pedestrians, loungers on benches, window shoppers, street preachers, food kiosks, and more.

At the same time, each element of the public realm can serve many functions. A street can accommodate traffic and then be closed off to host a greenmarket or a street fair or to become a route for bikers and joggers. A planting bed can serve as a catchment area for stormwater at the same time that it provides a home for plants that make the streetscape more attractive, provide shade in the summer, and host wildlife. A park can be a refuge from the city or a hub of activity. For example, in the summer, New York's Bryant Park is transformed once a week from a green urban respite into an outdoor theater that shows free movies.

Over the past two years, my firm has worked on several projects that create a mixed-use, multifunction public realm. In 2004, we proposed a twenty-three-mile trail and transit loop for Atlanta called the Beltline Emerald Necklace. The Beltline plan is now moving forward under the leadership of Atlanta Mayor Shirley Franklin. Focusing on a ring of abandoned railroads, the Beltline will create a connected parks system of more than 2,000 acres, including 1,200 acres of new parkland. At the same time, the light rail line will connect to the MARTA subway system, thus linking forty-six neighborhoods by transit with the city's major destinations. People will be able to use the trails to go for a walk, or bike to work, or take the light rail line to a concert or regional park. Above all, the Beltline is creating a regional public realm framework for walkable, transit-oriented growth—and this in Atlanta, the city of highways and backyards.

In Prince George's County, Maryland, we are working on a neighborhood scale, creating a 150-acre park in the midst of new greenfield development. The property on which the park will be built has two creeks running through it, part of the Chesapeake Bay watershed. Maryland has been justifiably concerned about water quality in the Chesapeake. However, their way of protecting the water on our site was a classic example of single-function planning—"don't touch" buffer zones alongside the creeks.

There is no reason to be so narrow-minded—drainage, waterways, and recreation can all coexist. More than a century ago, Frederick Law Olmsted did just

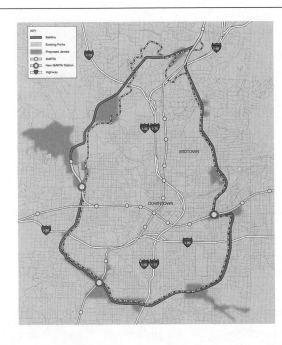

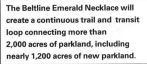

The Beltline Emerald Necklace will create a continuous trail and transit loop connecting more than 2,000 acres of parkland, including nearly 1,200 acres of new parkland.

Image courtesy of Alex Garvin & Associates

Bellwood Quarry was recently purchased by the city of Atlanta to become the city's largest park, one of the jewels of the Beltline Emerald Necklace. | Photo by Alex Garvin that in Boston's Back Bay Fens and Muddy River, which simultaneously provided flood control and an idyllic walkway. Decades later, his son, Frederick Law Olmsted Jr., made similar proposals in Boulder, Colorado, and Los Angeles for parks alongside flood-prone waterways. The Boulder Creek proposal was eventually implemented as part of a marvelous park system. The Los Angeles River proposal never made it off the shelf until, in recent years, angry citizens demanded that some of the forty-six miles of the concrete culvert that encases the Los Angeles River be transformed into the sort of public realm that Olmsted Jr. had envisioned decades earlier.

What we have proposed in Maryland is to dam the creeks and create a lake. The creeks leading into the lakes would be reconfigured to create ponding areas during floods. Scattered throughout the lakes would be small wetlands areas, and the lake would lead into a much larger wetland of several acres. Planted alongside the lake would be a wildlife corridor of native plants, providing habitat for native species and trails for humans.

The resulting ecosystem will filter the water, ensuring that it leaves the property cleaner than it entered it. It will provide habitats for birds and other animals and will restore a variety of native plant species. It will be able to handle stormwater runoff from surrounding development. At the same time, it will provide a superb recreational experience. People will be able to boat and swim in the lake, have coffee or a meal at a lakeside café, kayak or canoe through the wetland, take a walk through the reeds, birdwatch, animal watch, and more. Visiting schoolchildren will be able to learn about nature. None of these things would be possible if we left the creeks armored with untouchable buffers. Integrating these functions isn't just a better solution for people—it's a better solution for nature, people included.

The planning profession, along with money for planning, has been atrophying because planners haven't been proving their worth. As planners have turned more and more to regulating private property, they have been reduced to being bureaucratic functionaries, assigned to review and approve rezonings and subdivision plans. They are underfunded because the public is unconvinced of their worth.

We must revive the practice of strategic government investment. Planners must move beyond regulation to come up with positive new visions for the public realm. And they must figure out how to implement and pay for these visions.

Of course, that is the perennial question—how to pay for these things. There are two answers. The first is that strategic government investment is just that: an investment, which will yield returns in the long run. The investment is financed by government bonds, and the returns come in the form of increased tax revenues. This is how Central Park paid for itself and how Haussmann paid for the rebuilding of Paris. Today, the financial tools are more sophisticated, but the premise remains the same.

The second answer is that we are already making billions of dollars of investments in the public realm. These billions go to repave streets, repair sewers, renovate playgrounds, and update storefronts. This money will have to be spent, in one form or another.

This is the essence of planning—to ensure that the public funds are spent intelligently and efficiently and that they yield the most value possible. That value will come in the form of a great public realm, creating cities and suburbs that are safer, more attractive, and better places to live.

ALEXANDER GARVIN

has combined a career in urban planning and real estate with teaching, architecture, and public service. He is currently president and CEO of Alex Garvin & Associates Inc. He was managing director of Planning for NYC2012, New York City's committee for the 2012 Olympic bid, and was vice president for planning, design, and development at the Lower Manhattan Development Corporation, the agency charged with the redevelopment of the World Trade Center following 9/11. Over the past thirty-five years, Mr. Garvin held prominent positions in five New York City administrations, including deputy commissioner of housing and city planning commissioner. He is a professor of urban planning and management at Yale University, where he has taught for thirty-nine years.

MAKING BETTER PLACES:
TEN CITY DESIGN RESOLUTIONS

Jeff Speck |

With his experience leading the Mayors' Institute on City Design, Jeff Speck offers advice to city mayors who want to build better places.

America's cities are changing every day. Some are becoming better places to live; some, worse. Cities improve or worsen as a result of many intersecting forces, but if any one person has the ability to lead this change—or at least exert an influence—it is the American mayor.

One of the best unheralded programs of the National Endowment for the Arts is the Mayors' Institute on City Design. For almost twenty years, this group has been putting mayors together with designers to rethink the shape of their cities. After I have spent eighteen months working with this program, a number of design truisms that I once understood mostly in theory have become painfully obvious in practice. That many of these items are common sense does not alter the fact that mayors every day make decisions large and small that violate them outright. So, for all the mayors today who want to make better places, and for the citizens who want to help, I offer the following ten City Design Resolutions. Those who wish to call them commandments are welcome to do so.

1. Design Streets for People

What attracts people to cities? For most, it is the public realm, with the vibrant street life that phrase implies. A successful public realm is one that people can inhabit comfortably on foot. Unfortunately, most cities today still allow their streets to be designed by traffic engineers who ignore the real needs of pedestrians. For example, parallel parking, essential to protecting people on the sidewalk, is commonly eliminated to speed the traffic. Every aspect of the streetscape, including lane widths, curbs, sidewalks, trees, and lighting, can be designed to the needs of either cars or people. Too many cities favor the former.

Design streets for people: a street designed for cars—and drainage—but not for walking.
Photo courtesy of Duany Plater-Zyberk and Company

2. Overrule the Specialists

Engineers are not alone in their quest to shape the city around specialized needs. The modern world is full of experts who are paid to ignore criteria beyond their profession. But the specialist is the enemy of the city, which is by definition a general enterprise. The school and parks departments will push for fewer, larger facilities, since these are easier to maintain. The public works department will insist that new neighborhoods be designed principally around snow and trash removal. The department of transportation will build new roads to ease traffic generated by the very sprawl that they cause. Each of these approaches may be correct in a vacuum, but each is wrong in a city. Cities need generalists like mayors to weigh the advice of specialists against the common good.

3. Mix the Uses

Another key to active street life is creating a twenty-four-hour city, with neighborhoods so diverse in use that they are occupied around the clock. Eating, shopping, working, socializing—these activities are mutually reinforcing and flourish in the presence of the others. Moreover, many businesses, such as restaurants and health clubs, rely on both daytime and evening traffic to cover their rent. When considering the future of any city district, the first step should be to ask what uses are missing. In many downtowns, the answer to that question is housing, and cities from Providence to San Diego can point to new housing as a big part of a recent turnaround. In his book *Up from Zero* (Random House, 2004), Paul Goldberger is completely accurate in bemoaning the main error of the World Trade Center redesign planning process: its failure to introduce any housing into those sixteen commercial acres.

4. Hide the Parking Lots

If they are to keep walking, pedestrians must feel safe, comfortable—and entertained. And nothing is more boring than a parking lot. Whether they are open-air or six stories tall, parking lots must be banished along any street that hopes to attract walking. Happily, parking lots are easy to hide. It takes only a twenty-foot-thick crust of housing or offices to block a huge lot from view, and new parking structures can easily be built atop ground-level shops. Smart cities across the country are putting this requirement into law. Is yours?

Hide the parking lots: a garage in Miami Beach squeezes behind historic storefronts. | Photo by Jeff Speck

5. Small is Beautiful

People are small, and the most walkable cities acknowledge this fact with small blocks, small streets, small buildings, and small increments of investment. Portland, Oregon, owes much of its success to its tiny blocks, which create an incredibly porous network of streets, each of which can be quite small as a result. Whether for the megablock housing schemes of the 1960s or the cul-de-sac craze of the 1980s, most cities that have closed streets in the past now wish they hadn't.

Building height is another place for smallness. Only in the densest cities, where land doesn't sit empty as parking lots, are tall buildings justified. Otherwise, allowing skyscrapers just causes a few lucky sites to become overbuilt while their neighbors all lay fallow under massive speculation. Limiting building heights is also a useful bargaining chip: only with a height limit in place can height bonuses then be offered as an incentive for other concessions. Finally, do not tie the fate of your city to a single corporate juggernaut with its silver-bullet megamall when you should instead be leading the way for the local investor who wants to renovate a rowhouse.

6. Save That Building

How many buildings do we need to tear down before we learn our lesson? Almost every city that deeply regrets the 1960s destruction of its 1900s structures is happily permitting the 2000s destruction of 1940s structures. Need the march of time only confirm our current ignorance? Historic preservation may be our best way to respect our ancestors, but it is also justified on economic terms alone. Don Rypkema reminds us that in market economies, it is the differentiated product that commands a monetary premium ("Culture, Historic Preservation and Economic Development in the 21st Century," paper submitted to the Leadership Conference on Conservancy and Development, September 1999). This is why cities like Savannah and Miami Beach can point to historic preservation as the key ingredient in their recent booms. It isn't always easy to find a productive use for an empty old building, but tearing it down makes that outcome impossible. In these cases, remember the old adage: "Don't do something; just stand there!"

7. Build (Normal) Affordable Housing

Affordable housing remains a crisis in most cities, but the solution is not to build more housing projects. Rather, to be successful, affordable housing must do two things: (1) be integrated with market-rate housing and (2) look like market-rate housing. The most effective affordability programs combine housing with preservation by building city-owned houses on "missing tooth" empty lots in struggling historic neighborhoods. These houses provide smaller-than-standard apartments, but they are stylistically compatible with their neighbors. Despite the best-intentioned efforts of three generations of architecture students, affordable housing is exactly the wrong place to pioneer new design styles. Experiment on the rich; they can always move out.

Build (normal) affordable housing: Charleston, South Carolina has eliminated all new housing projects in favor of compatible infill construction.

Photo courtesy of
City of Charleston, South Carolina

8. Build Green and Grow Green

People have been talking about sustainable architecture for decades, but that movement has finally hit the tipping point with the advent of the U.S. Green Building Council's LEED (Leadership in Energy and Environmental Design) standards. There is no longer any excuse for not building green. The standards allow a building to become certified as sustainable in terms of its resource use and interior health. It costs a little bit more to build green, but these costs are made up quickly in energy savings and worker productivity. Chicago and Seattle are two of many cities that now require all municipal buildings to be LEED certified. Does yours? Oh, and while we're on the subject of green: plant more trees! If mayors understood the correlation between tree cover and real estate value, our cities would look like forests.

9. Question Your Codes

A "dingbat" is an apartment house on stilts floating above an exposed parking lot. The construction of one dingbat on a street of elegant rowhouses is enough to send property values plummeting. Why, then, do most city codes make no distinction between rowhouses and dingbats? Conventional zoning codes, made up of incomprehensible statistics like floor area ratios, ignore the differences between pleasant and unbearable urbanism. More often than not, they also make a city's traditional urban form—short front setbacks and mixed uses—illegal to emulate. For these reasons, a new generation of design ordinances is gaining favor among planners. Called *form-based code*, these ordinances regulate what really matters: a building's height, disposition, location, and where it puts the parking. These codes actually have pictures in them—imagine! Cities including Arlington, Virginia, and Miami are creating form-based codes for key neighborhoods. Governor Arnold Schwarzenegger just signed a bill encouraging form-based codes in California. What does the Arnold know that your city doesn't?

Question your codes: these two housing types, the "dingbat" seen to the left and the apartment villa on page 86, are statistically equivalent in most codes.

Photo courtesy of Duany Plater-Zyberk and Company/Jeff Speck

Photo courtesy of Duany Plater-Zyberk and Company/Jeff Speck

10. Don't Forget Beauty

Charleston Mayor Joe Riley reminds us that cities should be places that make the heart sing. For many of our citizens, especially those too poor or infirm to travel, the city is an entire world. For this reason, it is our responsibility to create and maintain cities that not only function properly but also offer moments of beauty. Yet how many communities today routinely award to the lowest bidder their contracts for schools, parks, and government buildings, the only investments that belong to us all? In the interest of short-term parsimony, we cheat ourselves out of an honorable public realm and a noble legacy. This was not always the case, and it need not continue. Many of the nation's most beautiful buildings and parks were built during periods of unparalleled adversity. It should not take another depression to make civic structures lovely again.

Cities are the largest and most complex things that we humans make. Despite evidence to the contrary, the knowledge exists on how to make them well. To the mayors—and citizens—who want to create better places, please start here.

JEFF SPECK,

a city planner, was director of design at the National Endowment for the Arts, where he oversaw the Mayors' Institute on City Design until stepping down in May 2007. He is co-author with Andrés Duany and Elizabeth Plater-Zyberk of *Suburban Nation: The Rise of Sprawl and the Decline of the American Dream* (New York: North Point Press, 2000).

This article was originally published by Planetizen on January 10, 2005.

RESPONSES FROM READERS

Local Distinctiveness and Individuality

From a United Kingdom point of view—a small country with sky-high property prices and land values and lots of history—the resolutions are most reminiscent of the CittaSlow movement, started in Italy. I know that at least its parent, the Slow Food (i.e., as opposed to fast food) movement has reached the United States. The key is local distinctiveness: keep your individuality, and keep the corporations and the faceless developers at bay. Don't build malls; cherish your small shopkeepers, gallery owners, and local restaurants, and so forth. You'll improve the quality of life for residents and be more appealing to visitors at the same time, as well as safeguarding the environment. And read Jane Jacobs's *The Death and Life of Great American Cities*—she said it all in the 1960s. If only the planners had listened then. —*January 16, 2005*

Resolution Revised

These resolutions, as the author says, are reincarnations of a "number of design truisms," and therein lies the trap. Truisms are often repeated because they sound so commonsensical, but, surprisingly, they are not always as sensible as they seem. Take for example #1: Design Streets for People.

What attracts people to cities? The story of urbanization says: jobs, jobs, jobs, and then opportunity and "urbanity" (another word for tolerance and lifestyle choice). In New York, L.A., Bangkok, Tokyo, Paris, and London, there are probably more bad streets than good, but these cities keep luring people to them. Streets don't register on the radar of common people choosing a city as their destiny.

A successful public realm? Streets are only one part of the public realm and a very small part at that. Squares (small and big), parks, trails, promenades, pubs, cafés, stadiums, arenas, theaters, train and subway stations, conference centers, stock exchange halls, farmers' markets, open and enclosed malls are all elements of the permanent or transient public realm that livens a city. The greater their frequency, the more vibrant the city. Let us then not ignore 90 percent of the real "public realm" by focusing exclusively on streets, the majority of which are rarely "inhabited." On these grounds #1 becomes: let there be many people places.

Streets for cars or people? It depends. Both need to move; both need to connect; both want to be safe. Streets have many faces, and not every face fits every role—highways, parkways, regional roads, main strips, main streets, local streets, mews, and lanes, to name just a few. Each of these suits the car or the pedestrian to differing degrees; some even exclude one or the other with good reason. The best people streets exclude cars (in many downtowns), and the best car streets bar pedestrians (most highways). Pick your master and design appropriately.

A Portland model? The "porous" plan of Portland uses about 43 percent of land for right-of-way and a corresponding amount of asphalt—neither a developer's ideal nor an environmentalist's dream. A five-minute walk means crossing up to ten motor streets, almost one quarter of the trip on asphalt—not exactly the ideal, carefree, socially stimulating stroll.

With these additional grounds, Resolution 1 becomes: Let there be many people places and as exclusively for people as possible.   —*January 18, 2005*

AUTHOR'S RESPONSE

In the comment "Resolutions Revised," the commenter is right that I should not have said "truisms" in describing these lessons. Rather, I should have said "truths"—that's how confident I am in them.

That said, every one of my points is intentionally a simplification intended to push conventional planning practice in the direction it needs to go—back toward a more livable city. The commenter is absolutely correct in stating that we need streets for cars, people, and everything in between. What he fails to acknowledge is that we have a problem: our streets, more often than not, speed vehicles at the expense of the pedestrian. In calling for narrower lanes, parallel parking, vertical curbs, street trees, and ample sidewalks, I am not saying we don't also need highways. I am simply trying to push a very biased system back a bit toward one in which the pedestrian has a fighting chance.

There are a number of other comments above that I take issue with but, for the sake of brevity, I will not dispute them. Let's just say that those of us who design streets for a living do not agree that "streets don't register on the radar of common people." On the contrary, we get out of bed every morning because we know in our hearts that the quality of the public realm—which in America is mostly streets—has a profound impact on the quality of our lives.

—September 2006

PRINCIPLES ESSENTIAL TO THE RENEWAL OF ARCHITECTURE

Andrés Duany |

The co-founder of the Congress for the New Urbanism outlines forty-one principles to reorient the practice of architecture toward the purity of good design.

In response to an age rife with social stress, driven by economies so powerful that the entirety of the natural world is decisively affected by the pattern of human dwelling, for a design profession confused by the esoteric and the transient, we who agree to sign this manifesto set forth these principles:

It is essential that the discipline of architecture take substance from its own tradition and not be subjected to artistic or intellectual fashions. Architecture is not a consumer item.

It is essential that the language of architecture be in continual evolution but not fall under the subjugation of short fashion cycles.

It is essential that architecture interact with the imperatives of economics and marketing but not be consumed by them. It is a role of the art of architecture to tame the savagery of commerce.

It is essential that architecture engage the supporting disciplines of engineering and sociology but not be enslaved by them.

It is essential that certain critics—those who do not possess the craft and experience of building—not be granted undue influence on the reputation of architecture and architects.

It is essential that architects develop an unmediated voice in the press to explain their work themselves. (Architects should effect this demand by canceling their subscriptions to those publications that do not comply.)

It is essential to observe that participation in a permanent avant-garde is an untenable position that consumes those who try to participate. Architects at the peak of their abilities must not be marginalized merely because their time of fame has passed.

It is essential to eliminate the humiliation of architects performing for the opinion of an absurdly small number of critics. Such critics are empowered only because they are recognized as such by the architects themselves. This problem does not apply to architectural historians, who earn their standing through research and documentation rather than through personal preference. Historians support the knowledge base on which architecture stands and from which it evolves.

It is essential that buildings be durable and mutable in balanced measure. This is crucial to the longevity required of urbanism.

It is essential that the design schools accept the responsibility of teaching a body of knowledge and not attempt to incite individualism. Students should be exposed to the general vernacular and not just to the very few geniuses produced by each generation. Emulation of the exceptional does not provide an adequate model for professional training.

It is essential that the architectural schools be liberated from the thrall of sociologists, linguists, and philosophers. Those who are primarily dedicated to other disciplines should return to their own departments from which they can continue to educate architects in proper measure.

It is essential that the wall between history and the design studio be eliminated. History is to be a living continuum. The achievements of our predecessors are the foundation for all future human progress. Architecture cannot be the sole exception.

It is essential that students be exposed to the apprenticeship system. There is no more effective method of learning architecture. Most of the finest buildings of all time were the result of apprenticeship.

It is essential to our communities that architecture be practiced as a collective endeavor and not as a means of brand differentiation in pursuit of the attentions of the media.

It is essential that architects retake responsibility for an urbanism that is currently abandoned to the statistical concerns of zoning, building codes, traffic, and financing.

It is essential that architectural expression assimilate the cultural and climatic context no less than it assimilates the will to form of the architect.

It is essential that buildings acknowledge the character of a place. It is also necessary to acknowledge the opposite: that architectural influence can travel along cultural and climatic belts to positive effect.

It is essential that architecture not become a pawn in the culture wars. It is a falsification of history to consider a style representative of a particular hegemony or liberation.

It is essential to see that architectural style is independent of politics. The most cursory observation will reveal that buildings and cities are neither democratic nor fascist, that they easily transcend the ideology of their creators to become useful and beloved to other inhabitants and eras.

It is essential that buildings incorporate authentic progress in material and production methods but not for the sake of innovation alone.

It is essential that architects harness those systems of production that make the best design available to the greatest number. Only those artifacts that are reproduced in quantity are consequential to present needs—we face the challenge of large numbers.

It is essential that the techniques of mass production affect the process of building, but it is not necessary that they determine the form of the building, or the urbanism.

It is essential to engage the mobile home industry, the prefabrication industry, and the house plan industry. These industries present efficient methods for providing housing. The current low quality of their production is the fault of nonparticipation by architects.

It is essential that architects endeavor to publish their work in popular periodicals. How else will the people learn?

It is essential that the techniques of graphic depiction not determine the design of the buildings. Computer-aided design must remain an instrument for the liberation of labor and not become a determinant of form. Because a shape can be easily depicted does not necessarily mean that it should be constructed.

It is essential to recognize that each building should be coherently composed. A building cannot be the simulacrum of an absent urbanism. Authentic variety can only result from a multiplicity of buildings. True urbanism is the result of many designers working in sequence.

It is essential that traditional and contemporary architectural styles have equal standing, as they represent parallel, persistent realities. They may be used badly or well, but their evaluation should be on the basis of their quality and their appropriateness to context, not to fashion.

It is essential to deny contemporary buildings dispensation for having been created in the so-called Modernist era. They must be held to a standard as high as their predecessors. After all, the means available currently are not less than those available in the past.

It is essential to acknowledge a preference for controls by known rules and properly constituted laws, rather than be subjected to the whims and opinions of review boards.

It is essential that architects work concurrently with landscape architects in the process of design. Landscape architects must in turn abdicate their preference for autonomous layouts. The ground is not a canvas, and nature is not material suitable for an installation piece.

It is essential that architects, like attorneys, dedicate a portion of their time without compensation to those who do not otherwise have access to professional design. It is essential that architects participate in the political arena so as to affect the built environment at the largest scale. It is disastrous to create policy without the participation of those with an adequate design education.

It is essential that architects debate those who, through relativist argument, undermine architecture's potential as a social and ecological instrument for the good. The academic imperative of weakening architecture and architects harms society.

It is essential that we not impose untested or experimental designs on the poor. The likelihood of failure in such cases has proven to be very great; the poor are powerless to escape its consequences. Architects should experiment, if at all, with those wealthy enough to be patrons. They can afford to move out of their buildings, if necessary.

It is essential to understand the difference between creativity, which we accept as a necessity, and originality, which when pursued at all costs is destructive to architecture. The pursuit of originality condemns our cities to incoherence and the architect's life's work to unwarranted obsolescence.

Because so much of the craft of building has been lost, it is essential that architects allocate a portion of their time to its research and recovery and to the sharing of the fruits of this endeavor by teaching and writing.

It is essential that the architectural vernaculars of the world be the subjects of systematic study and that they be models for the design process. Good, plain, normative buildings must again be available everywhere and to all.

It is essential that the analysis of everyday buildings not result in the conclusion that the people will accept only mediocrity. It is pandering to give them only what they already know.

It is essential that buildings incorporate passive environmentalism in siting, materials, and the performance of their mechanical elements. Economic analysis alone will not reach this conclusion.

It is essential that architectural history include not just the form givers but the masters of policy. Talented students who are not seduced by form making should be exposed to these role models. Municipal policy and administration is sorely in need of their abilities.

It is essential that architects respond to context. If the context is not suitable, then the proper response is to inaugurate one that is. Not until this is common practice will the proliferation of architectural review committees cease to bedevil both good and bad designers.

ANDRÉS DUANY, FAIA,

is a principal of Duany Plater-Zyberk & Company. He is a co-founder and member of the Congress for the New Urbanism.

This article was originally published by Planetizen on September 23, 2003.

RESPONSES FROM READERS

Need Room for Input

A significant omission from these principles is the opportunity for meaningful public input in the design of buildings. City planners already know the importance of allowing citizens of a community to provide direction regarding the development of their community, and design of structures should not be an exception. Architects practice a craft whose results affect the entirety of an area. The public, therefore, is the ultimate client of any architect and should be considered as such.   —*September 16, 2003*

WHY NEW URBANISM FAILS

Christopher DeWolf

Behind their quaint, cozy façades, New Urbanist towns still fail to combat the pattern of sprawling, autocentric suburban development.

Since the early 1990s, New Urbanism has slowly gathered strength, a building storm that finally burst into the American mainstream only a few years ago. Its "neotraditional" principles—wide sidewalks and narrow streets, front porches and rear garages, central squares and shopping districts—garnered attention across Canada and the United States. Some of the communities that resulted tried to emulate small towns, while others resembled urban neighborhoods. In the end, however, their goal was the same: create new developments that are community- and people-oriented.

Unfortunately, as popular and seemingly positive as these developments are, they fail in their objective and ultimately reinforce the strength of the auto-oriented suburban environment. They are feel-good faux towns, cozy and nostalgic developments that feign urbanity without making the effort to actually be urban.

One of the fundamental tenets of the New Urbanism is the reinforcement of community life. This is why lots are smaller, houses are closer to the street, sidewalks are plentiful, and garages are banished to the rear of the houses. This, in theory, allows neighbors to chat and say hello while strolling down the street to fetch some milk at the corner store. Many New Urbanist developments are separated into small segments, each with its own central focus—a square, perhaps—and a small grocery store. Downtown main streets are also vital to the New Urbanist ideology. Ideally, they are concentrations of vital retail services, restaurants, and cafés where people from around the neighborhood can bump into one another on broad sidewalks.

In keeping with the concept of traditional design, residential areas typically contain architecture meant to resemble that of small towns. Brick townhouses, white picket fences, and Colonial homes abound, sometimes creating a contrived atmosphere that seems less like a real neighborhood and more like a television set. As Michael Sorkin wrote in the September 1998 issue of *Metropolis* magazine: "New Urbanism reproduces many of the worst aspects of the Modernism it seeks to replace; [it] promotes another style of universality that is similarly over reliant on visual cues to produce social effects" (from "Acting Urban" September 1998, *Metropolis Magazine*). Instead of actually being successful urban neighborhoods, New Urbanist developments simply look like urban neighborhoods.

New Urbanist developments may be aesthetically pleasing, but aesthetics alone do not create community or urbanity. New Urbanist towns too often commit the most heinous of urban sins: they segregate zones. Certainly, it is not uncommon to find small commercial outlets in the residential quarters of neotraditional developments, but by and large these neighborhoods follow the standard planning principle of the past fifty years, which is to distinctly separate zones according to use. The majority of commercial establishments are constricted to designated town centers surrounded by a ring of residential areas with few bridges to connect the two sections. This zone segregation keeps New Urbanist communities from resembling the small towns and urban neighborhoods they strive to become. They lack the organic growth and fluid blend of multiple uses that make urban neighborhoods so successful.

The problem with segregated zones is that a reliance on the automobile is constructed just as it is in normal suburban areas. Since town centers are often too far out of easy walking distance from many homes, cars are needed for a trip to buy groceries or to rent a video. The results are town centers that seem like inverse strip malls, with pedestrian-friendly Main Streets lined by charming buildings (governed by strict architectural controls) yet with large parking lots behind. Jane Jacobs noted in an interview with James Howard Kunstler that "the notion of a shopping center as a valid kind of downtown has taken over. It's very hard for architects of this generation even to think in terms of a downtown that is owned by different people with different ideas (from "Godmother of the American City," March 2001, *Metropolis Magazine*). Similarly, she stated in an interview with *Reason Magazine* that "the New Urbanists want to have lively centers, [yet] they don't seem to have a sense of the anatomy of these hearts" (from "City Views," June 2001, *Reason Magazine*). In New Urbanism, the strip mall is designed quaintly, with parking out of sight and building aesthetics governed by developer- or community-set controls. This is not an acceptable alternative to a real town center.

One of North America's largest New Urbanist developments is McKenzie Towne in Calgary, Alberta. Located several miles from the downtown area, McKenzie Towne embodies all the flaws I see in modern New Urbanism: segregated zones, an inadvertent reliance on the car, a contrived atmosphere. And while the original section of the development contains a variety of mixed-density housing, it was recently announced that new sections separate housing types from one another—yet another similarity between standard suburbia and New Urbanist suburbia. Wendell Cox, a staunch critic of the New Urbanism, said it best when he wrote on his website called "Calgary's McKenzie Towne: Suburb with a Neo-Traditional Façade," that beneath McKenzie Towne's neotraditional exterior "beats the heart of suburbia" (at www.demographia.com/db-mckenzietowne.htm).

What disturbs me most about the popularity of the New Urbanism is that it has led us to neglect the old urbanism. What is wrong with the organic neighborhoods that fill inner cities? They never stopped working, as countless metropolises can attest. Most New Urbanist neighborhoods are greenfield developments built without context on urban peripheries. Many lack adequate transit service to existing urban neighborhoods, standing alone in a vacuum of more typical subdivisions. New Urbanism tries to fool us into believing it is the savior of urbanity when in reality it is nothing more than a new style of slipshod suburban development. It is a pretty veil over common suburbia.

Christopher DeWolf

lives in Montreal, where he is a writer, a photographer, and the editor of Urbanphoto.net, a website dedicated to exploring the urban environment through photography.

This article was originally published by Planetizen on February 18, 2002.

RESPONSES FROM READERS

Why New Urbanism Prevails

Starting a reform effort is a hazardous business. You might have the greatest ideals in the world, but should you ever fall short of perfection—beware! Naysayers and critics leap up at the first opportunity, well-stocked with "I told you so" and "Shame on you."

In fact, New Urbanism works for many of the same goals as Mr. DeWolf. He writes: "Most New Urbanist neighborhoods are greenfield developments built without context on urban peripheries." Well, no. The truth is that fully 50 percent of New Urban developments were infill in 2001, according to the industry journal *New Urban News*. Leaders in the movement have been at the forefront of reform in federal public housing design standards, creating numerous successful neighborhoods in the United State's central cities. Other New Urbanists are deeply involved in downtown redevelopment planning, mixed-use apartment towers, and smaller projects that reknit neighborhoods shredded by highways and car-centric megastructures.

Yes, many New Urban developments lack the ideal mix of uses and housing types. Sometimes, sad to say, they are designed that way from the get-go. So, buyer beware! Don't be gullible: just because a development calls itself New Urban doesn't mean it really is.

However, New Urban projects are sometimes designed well but executed poorly. In some cases, the municipality derails the designer's intentions. Sometimes the banks or developers reject mixed use and mixed income as money-losing propositions. But give these developments time—most are only a few years old. Many have a form and infrastructure that will, over the years, provide the capacity to evolve and improve—just as every great city in the world has.

And what of the suburbs? For all his complaints, Mr. DeWolf has not provided a credible alternative to New Urbanism on the urban fringe. Should we ban all greenfield growth? It's not possible in the United States. Even Portland's growth boundary expands to accommodate new projects. In fact, more than 95 percent of new growth occurs at the urban fringe. To simply abandon the fringe to standard suburbia is to give up entirely on the sprawl battle. It is the New Urban neighborhoods that establish the walkable, transit-accessible kernels for better patterns of growth.   —*February 18, 2002*

Less Defense of Movement, More Movement

So often one hears people defend movements by claiming that any negative aspects are just imperfect copies of the ideal.

The truth is that downtown infill projects, whether they are designed by New Urbanists or not, are just simply urban projects whose merit can be judged by urban design standards that were preexistent to the New Urbanists and are practiced by a variety of denominations of urban designers and architects. One simply has to look at the unplanned prewar urban areas of most central urban areas in North America to see examples of dense, mixed-use, Main Street, pedestrian-friendly urban areas that were once suburbs. Some aspects of New Urbanist rhetoric improve on the prewar suburbs, such as their aspirations in environmental issues, but these aspirations have been simultaneously developed in other urban theories and movements and are not unique to New Urbanism.

What is unique to New Urbanist practice is its preponderance for spawning bad copies on greenfield sites, as Mr. DeWolf describes. Frankly, a movement should be judged by the quality of its bad copies, not by the idealism of its aspirations. The modern movement, as the New Urbanists often have demonstrated, has taught us that lesson.

The alternative to New Urban greenfield developments is not a movement. Movements by definition create ideals that will ultimately be badly copied. The alternative is for cities to take back the control of their rights-of-way from the development industry and ensure that all roads (especially arterial roads) are designed as civic places that are interconnected with the city rather than trans-portation diagrams. New Urbanists know how to do this on paper. If they spent less time defending their movement and more time saying no to developers and banks, maybe they wouldn't need a movement. Then they could be just simple "urbanists" with the rest of us.   —*February 19, 2002*

New Urbanism: A Rediscovery

Is it possible that there are lessons from neighborhoods that work that can be applied to today's developments? It is the very essence of the New Urbanist movement to find these elements and apply them in the context of today's social and fiscal realities. It's no easy job, as the shortcomings so appropriately pointed out demonstrate. Instead of banning New Urbanism to the trash heap, I suggest we encourage the valiant effort to rediscover and apply design and planning principles to our modern society. Admittedly, we have a ways to go. But let's support the effort and build on our successes and failures.

Let me also suggest that New Urbanist principles do not just relate to cities but also to whatever lifestyle or population density we apply to a community. Whether a rural agricultural environment, small village or town, or the most densely urban city, each has elements of design that are unique and make it function well for its inhabitants. And conversely, there are elements of design that are to be avoided if we care about a well-functioning community.

It is the intent of the New Urbanism movement to discover the principles that make for neighborhoods that "work" and apply them to today's development needs. As we try and learn, we will have relative successes and failures. But let's not discard the "movement" based on relative failure. Let's honor the effort and the learning that the movement is generating.   —*February 21, 2002*

AUTHOR'S RESPONSE

A more accurate (though certainly less provocative) title for my article would have been "*Where* New Urbanism Fails." When it was first published five years ago, many readers assumed I was attempting to launch a broad-based attack on New Urbanism. I wasn't. Rather, I was taking issue with the many suburban developments that called themselves New Urbanist but displayed some of the most basic characteristics of traditional postwar sprawl. Developments such as McKenzie Towne in Calgary are a nostalgic veneer over ordinary suburbs. Even with their front porches, quaint architecture, back alleys, and token corner stores, they do not function much differently than regular suburbia: most of their inhabitants still drive to work, still shop at large-format retail stores, and still do not engage in the public sphere beyond walking their dog through the neighborhood park.

This is not to say that New Urbanism has failed outright. In fact, it should be pointed out that it is the failure of individual developments to adhere to the Charter of the New Urbanism, which contains an admirable list of characteristics that are present in almost every successful neighborhood. Many New Urbanist developments that are built on greenfield sites near highway exits—which is to say a very large number of them—fail to achieve even the most basic of these elements, such as developing transit corridors, building at densities high enough to encourage pedestrian activity, finely mixing uses, and seamlessly integrating new developments into their surroundings. Far too often, New Urbanist developments are compromised by low density, a complete lack of adequate public transit, and suburban intrusions such as big-box supermarkets. Worse, they often fall into the trap of becoming irrelevant bastions of nostalgic living for the upper middle class, where cafés and florists are within walking distance but the everyday essentials of life are always a drive away.

What's needed is a shift in focus away from reshaping new suburban development and toward the redevelopment of first-ring suburban areas and urban brownfields. Some of the best examples of New Urbanist principles employed in new development can be found in Vancouver and Portland, where vacant land adjacent to the central business district has been redeveloped with high-density apartment buildings, towers, and townhouses. In Vancouver, nearly twenty thousand people now live on a former waterfront railyard in a neighborhood that is pedestrian- and transit-oriented, visually appealing, mixed-use, and home to a diverse range of inhabitants, including the poor (thanks to social housing) and many families (thanks to large apartments). Over the past six years, this high-density development has brought six new urban-format supermarkets to downtown Vancouver, and it has led to a dramatic decrease in the number of cars that circulate in the downtown core.

If New Urbanism expects to remain relevant, it has to destroy the stale reputation it has earned in recent years, one that is based on the perception that it is hopelessly quaint, impractical, and ineffective. There are plenty of examples of New Urbanism that work—they just can't be found in the fantasyland finish of many failed developments. *—September 2006*

URBAN PARKS: INNOVATE OR STAGNATE

Fred Kent

If the majority of America's parks are to avoid stagnation, they need to learn from those parks that are getting it right.

Massive budget cuts in U.S. cities, combined with a growing focus on urban revitalization and walkable cities, has put urban parks in the spotlight as never before. Effectiveness is the name of the game, and however you look at it, there's no doubt that the most effective parks are the ones that are best used.

But it is not just a matter of attracting lots of people; it's a matter of having a diversity of people who are attracted by a range of things to do throughout the year.

This is why it is so remarkable that, although people profess to love parks, many parks are failing to attract people. Take a look for yourself in towns and cities across the country, and you'll see parks and plazas galore that have little happening in them.

The problem is that we seem to be losing the art of successful park design and management. Basic elements, such as comfort, sociability, access, and activities, seem to have slipped through the cracks as more and more parks fail to meet the mixed and varied needs of their visitors.

Even high-profile parks are showing signs of being in trouble. New York's Bryant Park—famed for a renovation that brought crowds to a once-derelict hangout for drug dealers—is one example. While its lush lawns and convenient movable chairs make it a heavily used place for much of the year, it is increasingly given over to private interests. At the main park entrance, Starbucks has taken the place of local coffee purveyors. And the park is virtually inaccessible to regular folk for up to a month each year because of the semiannual Mercedes-Benz New York Fashion Week (including setup and recovery). Despite its innovative history, Bryant Park has become a victim of its own success and is cutting itself off from the public it ought to be serving.

While Bryant Park suffers as a result of corporatization, Denver's Skyline Park has been condemned because of overdesign and then abandonment. Described by *Rocky Mountain News* editor and publisher John Temple as a "bold vision, but flawed," the 3.2-acre park was completed in 1973 with the aim of renewing a blighted area of the city. The problem is that the sole path through the park goes nowhere, offering only concrete walls and ledges for comfort. Overflowing garbage cans, cigarette butts, and chipped wooden benches are a clear sign of a park that got left behind. (It's now slated for a controversial redesign.)

Granted, most parks are not at the epicenter of Midtown Manhattan, nor are they as dramatically neglected as Skyline Park. But it's not just the high-profile places that are at risk. Nibbled away for parking lots and office blocks, hijacked by single-issue recreational groups from dog owners to Little Leaguers, overdesigned by the very people trying to save them—America's everyday parks are also facing challenges.

So which ones are getting it right? They are the ones that have dedicated people who are willing to think creatively, innovate, and listen to their range of users.

The annual Flower Sale is one of hundreds of events held each year at Portland's Pioneer Courthouse Square.
Photo courtesy of Project for Public Spaces

It's always inspiring to look outside the United States for examples, such as at the Paris Plage, a smash hit in the summer of 2002. With a ribbon of sand, umbrellas, cafés, and volleyball courts, Mayor Bertrand Delano temporarily transformed 3.8 kilometers of inner-city expressway along the Seine River into an urban beach (displacing hundreds of thousands of motorists in the process). Seventeen city agencies worked together to create this temporary park, equipped with 80 imported palm trees, 22 changing tents, 150 parasols, and 300 blue canvas deck chairs.

Besides all these accoutrements, there was plenty to do at Paris Plage, including a string of cafés, music and dance floors, climbing walls, volleyball, *boules*, and putting greens. Despite the Paris Plage's taking place during the dog days of summer, when Paris empties, 3 million people visited in its first week, six hundred thousand on the first day alone.

The innovative Paris Plage event along the Seine (2002) has expanded the notion of what constitutes a park.
Photo courtesy of Project for Public Spaces

Vienna's Rathaus/City Hall Park is another good example. Surrounded by some of the city's most treasured buildings, the park is one of the city's most popular destinations for locals and tourists alike. It is used year-round for concerts, festivals, markets, and even small-scale tennis tournaments, but the biggest draws are the Christmas markets, the ice rink in January, and the classical music film festival in summer.

Back in North America, Portland's Pioneer Courthouse Square is another example of a park that has won the support of its public. Rather than opting for a passive green space, the square is indeed a "pioneer" among a new generation of public spaces designed for a flexible range of uses and activities. It has a continuing tradition of citizen participation with thousands of community events held over the past decade and ongoing experimentation with new seasonal uses.

On the other hand, Dufferin Grove Park in Toronto, Canada, provides plenty of green space but is far from passive in its uses. Described as a "community center without a roof," the park rejected the stereotypical children's playground and opted instead for the kind of "equipment" that universally appeals to kids: water, sand, crafts, and even old pots and pans. For older people, there's a community oven for baking pizza and bread, a theater, an ice rink, a wading pool, a baseball diamond, a basketball court, chess, checkers, card playing—all within a setting of beautiful and abundant old shade trees.

Great parks are the key to more livable towns and cities. The tragedy is that if they aren't well-designed and managed, then they aren't properly used—and if they aren't used—then they simply go away or cease to become public spaces.

So if the majority of America's parks are to avoid stagnation, they're going to need to learn a thing or two from those parks that are getting it right—and get back to creating parks that are attractive and accessible to everyone who wishes to use them.

FRED KENT

is president of Project for Public Spaces in New York and a leading authority on revitalizing city spaces.

This article was originally published by Planetizen on April 14, 2003.

RESPONSES FROM READERS

Economically Essential

It's great to read an optimistic view of public parks. If their creation is becoming a more complicated science, this should not deter public demand and need for such urban spaces.

Designed innovatively, they offer opportunities to build community cultures and even relieve social tensions, build economic structure, and restore natural habitat.

I would argue that without investing in the "unbuilt" environment (of urban parks), the economic potential of the "built" environment cannot reach its highest levels. Parks are as much an economic essential as are other economic elements (housing, industry, commerce, services, transport systems, and so forth). Neglecting park spaces is penny-wise and pound-foolish. —*April 15, 2003*

Economics of Parks

What we have here is a bunch of assertions without reference to the literature on the economics of parks. The attractiveness of parks can be measured by their effect on adjacent housing values. By this standard, the most attractive parks are either small neighborhood parks or larger nature preserves where there is no activity at all. Houses right next to large, active parks tend to have lower values.

What is needed is modeling of park economics to replace bald assertions. Another point that must always be considered when planners are on the loose: Is the "success" of this or that planning idea just a fad or does it have permanence? Is it a solution or just the first stage of the next planner-induced problem?

—*April 17, 2003*

Our Parks Are Being Sold

I've witnessed one problem that Fred Kent addresses in his article. Basically, special interest groups have invaded our parks with the help of corporate marketing dollars. Many community park managers end up selling our parks to the highest bidder. In return, we end up with cellular phone towers, single-use parks, and private business camping out in our places of refuge. We went to the park in the first place to get away from these people and their guerilla marketing tactics. I hope we get smart and demand the return of the classical park, simply a place where anyone can seek refuge. —*April 29, 2003*

DISASTER PLANNING
Introduction by the Editors of Planetizen

The adage "Rome wasn't built in a day" is generally good to remember when considering the crawling pace of city planning and development. Although there are cases of explosive growth in areas, it's much more common for cities to evolve and grow incrementally. Therefore, many city and community plans envision timeframes of five, ten, or even twenty years.

Yet, in the aftermath of a disaster, the planning profession is called on to respond immediately to resurrect an area struck down by tragic events. Recent events, such as 9/11, the Iraq War, and Hurricane Katrina, have reemphasized the need for city planning to help cities recover from misfortune and to plan to help prevent such tragic events in the first place.

Earthquakes, floods, cyclones, and fires have all been responsible for catastrophic damage to major cities around the world—in some cases destroying them completely. Although technology has enabled modern cities to better predict and cope with the growing number of natural disasters, the staggering damage caused by the 2004 Asian tsunami and by Hurricane Katrina in 2005 demonstrate how vulnerable even large cities continue to be to nature's wrath.

In addition to natural disasters, cities must cope with human-caused catastrophes and devastation. Warfare, rioting, and acts of terrorism can equal or exceed the devastation caused by Mother Nature. Unintentional though it may be, even poorly thought out urban planning can put cities in undue jeopardy. Shortsighted planning has placed cities like New Orleans in unsuitable locations susceptible to natural disasters and without adequate protection against the likelihood of catastrophic events.

When a disaster occurs, the initial recovery period primarily involves ensuring the safety and welfare of residents, along with basic cleanup—bringing in food and shelter and moving rubble. However, the failure of some past reconstruction efforts demonstrates that plans for the replacement of damaged buildings and infrastructure must be put into motion at the same time as basic safety and welfare efforts. But even that may not be enough. We are coming to realize the importance of having disaster recovery plans in place before disaster strikes.

Planners involved in the task of reconstruction planning face a critical decision: rebuild a city or neighborhood as it was before, or use the destruction as an opportunity to replan an area according to new ideas about how to build cities. In post-Katrina New Orleans, this battle rages on. As the floodwaters receded, a host of planning experts and architects descended on the Gulf Coast, eager to help in the process of reconstruction. Innovative ideas for rebuilding housing—such as the Katrina cottage—have been cited as positive outcomes of this focused attention. However, controversy ensues about plans to redraw the boundaries of New Orleans to allow flood-prone areas—typically home to low-income, predominantly black communities—to be reclaimed as open space.

While the New Orleans of the future will surely be different from the city that existed prior to the storm, it seems that an important aspect of reconstruction is the psychological need for residents to restore what once existed. This dynamic has also been present during the debate over the World Trade Center site in New York. While some planners and architects openly question the wisdom of continuing to build megatowers that are easy targets for terrorists, there seems to be little respect for the idea of not rebuilding. Many New Yorkers continue to wait patiently for the day when the Manhattan skyline is restored, yet plans for the new Freedom Tower are still hampered by the emotion and politics involved in agreeing on a final design and a reluctance of many businesses to occupy the new structures.

To create a reconstruction process that facilitates a speedy recovery and acceptance by residents, planners are best advised to make serious and deliberate efforts to engage the public in the planning process. Long a major criticism of the planning process in all venues, the lack of public participation is especially problematic when planning for disaster recovery and rebuilding, given the trauma suffered by the residents of the community. Merely showcasing plans and taking comments at a few town hall meetings will not be enough to provide people with a real sense of ownership over plans to rebuild. Without such ownership, residents will end up feeling like victims of another disaster.

Aside from dealing with reconstruction, the other aspect where planning is involved is the prevention of disasters—or at least the prevention of the negative impacts of disasters. In many earthquake- and hurricane-prone areas, buildings are designed to withstand the forces of nature. However, with the increasing costs of disaster recovery, some experts are wondering whether cities should be built in such high-risk areas. The threat of global warming has some planners recognizing the consequences that our planet's changing climate might have on misfortunately placed urban areas, as well as the harmful effects our urban areas can have on the natural environment.

Following the tragic events of September 11, 2001, planners in the United States and around the world focused on reexamining how cities can be made safer from acts of terrorism. Yet some of the recommendations for terror-proofing cities have serious consequences for urbanism. Should gates, fences, and borders become the norm in our cities—even at the expense of the vibrant civic life that the profession seeks to create? And if the public feels unsafe being in dense, urban areas, can urbanism survive at all?

These are all important questions that will help to dictate how cities react to the threat of disasters and how they recover from these events when they occur. The following articles discuss some of the most important lessons learned from recent natural disasters and humanmade catastrophes. Armed with these lessons, cities and planners can be better prepared for civilization's inevitable conflicts with nature and itself.

RECOVERING NEW ORLEANS

Thomas J. Campanella

Very few cities in history have been completely and permanently destroyed, although a major catastrophe invariably alters a city's fate. What will it take to ensure the survival of New Orleans? And even if it makes it past Katrina, will the city be able to regain its authenticity and unique character?

Even before the floodwaters of Lake Pontchartrain stopped their lethal rise in the wake of Hurricane Katrina, questions about the fate of New Orleans began to fly like shingles in a storm. These touched nearly every aspect of urban planning theory and practice, making a whole range of hypotheticals suddenly as real as the nightly news. In the lead was a question as simple as it was profound: Would this great American city survive? Should New Orleans be rebuilt—all of it—in its original place and as before? Would it be grossly irresponsible for the government to resettle thousands of families in a city so prone to catastrophic flooding?

By the first few days of September 2005, it was looking more and more like New Orleans might not make it. It didn't help that the city's deputy police chief, Warren Riley, claimed on the national news that the Big Easy was "completely destroyed." Nor did the total evacuation of the drowned town—itself unprecedented in American history—paint a hopeful picture. As thousands fled the city, New Orleans was "left to the dead," as the *Atlanta Journal-Constitution* headline read on September 4. To top it off, journalist Joel Garreau penned an elegiac piece in the *Washington Post*, with the depressing (and misleading) title "A Sad Truth: Cities Aren't Forever" (September 11, 2005). Would the United States, for all its wealth and power and technological prowess, be the first modern nation to lose a city?

Lost cities are, in fact, a relative historical rarity. True, Atlantis remains unfound, let alone rebuilt. Pompeii and Herculaneum were buried permanently beneath the hot ejecta of Vesuvius in 79 A.D. Timgad was sacked by both the Vandals and the Berbers and was lost to history until archaeologists uncovered it in

A photo of the New Orleans area taken by the Landsat 5 satellite on September 7, 2005. Black floodwaters cover much of the city.

Photo courtesy of the United States Geological Survey Center for Earth Resources Observation and Science

the 1880s. Monte Albán, on the heights above the modern Mexican city of Oaxaca, flourished for two thousand years before the Spanish conquistadors crushed it for all time.

But these cities are the exceptions. Much more common in the annals of urban history are cities that have rebounded again and again from horrific devastation. The Romans leveled Carthage after the Third Punic War, salting it for good measure. But it was the Romans themselves who later resurrected the port city and turned it into an administrative hub for their African possessions; even today, Carthage persists as a suburb of Tunis. By about 1800, urban resilience becomes the rule. No major city in the past two hundred or so years has been completely destroyed, in spite of humankind's ever-increasing power to do so. There are only a handful of exceptions. St. Pierre, Martinique—the "Paris of the Antilles"—was annihilated by a volcanic eruption in 1902 and never rebuilt. Only one man survived, and only because he was locked in solitary confinement. But for every St. Pierre, there are a hundred cities that bounced back from catastrophic destruction.

The subject of urban resilience is one I explored with Lawrence J. Vale in an anthology entitled *The Resilient City: How Modern Cities Recover from Disaster*

(New York: Oxford University Press, 2005). Our comparative study revealed no short answers as to why urban sites in the modern age are rarely abandoned. Our study did yield, however, a number of key points and common themes about both disasters and urban resilience, many of which have gained new relevance in the wake of Hurricane Katrina. For one, cities vary enormously in their resilience. Just as some people can fend off an illness while others succumb, not all cities are equally capable of rebounding from a shock to the system.

A person whose health is compromised to begin with has less chance of recovery than an individual in full health. So, too, a city. New York proved highly resilient in the wake of 9/11, marshaling vast financial, political, and cultural capital in its effort to recover from the destruction of the World Trade Center. New Orleans, on the other hand, was already burdened with considerable socioeconomic problems before Katrina's arrival. Such "preexisting conditions" will play a major role in determining how well the Crescent City will recover from the storm and its aftermath—and perhaps whether it can recover at all.

Urban resilience, moreover, is not necessarily progressive. In spite of the seeming *tabula rasa* opportunity a major disaster offers to correct old errors and put things right, reconstruction tends to favor the status quo. Even if a city's buildings are toppled, foundations and embedded infrastructure are often reusable, and property boundaries can usually be reconstructed from archival documents. The imperatives of insurance policies, combined with simple inertia, push many landowners to rebuild more or less what they lost. There is also a deep psychological need to put things quickly back the way they were. While a disaster can be a catalyst for long-term innovations, its immediate aftermath is often a time of cautiousness and conservatism, officially at least.

This is why bold new plans rarely get implemented following a catastrophe; they're a luxury for times of peace and are usually promoted by visiting visionaries with little at stake personally. In London after the Great Fire of 1666, grand plans by Christopher Wren, John Evelyn, and others remained paper dreams, defeated by "a complicated system of freeholds, leases and subleases," to quote Kevin Lynch. London was rebuilt largely as before. And although Chicago's Great Fire of 1871 led in time to a city of fireproof masonry architecture and the world's first skyscrapers, initial rebuilding utilized the very kinds of firetrap construction that had caused the catastrophe in the first place. There are exceptions, of course; an authoritarian regime, unencumbered by democracy, can dictate a city's reconstruction. When the Chinese government rebuilt Tangshan, leveled by an earthquake in 1976, it was a modern industrial city that barely resembled its tumbledown predecessor.

This notion of "regressive resilience" extends also to a city's social order and political culture. Just as the built environment is commonly reconstituted as before, the power structure and social hierarchy of a city can quickly replicate itself in the wake of a catastrophe. Divisive predisaster social inequities and injustices are resilient too. On the other hand, nothing reveals the fault lines in a society like a major calamity, exposing to public scrutiny long-hidden patterns of power, poverty, race, and class. Such exposure can, in the right circumstances, precipitate positive change. This was the case in Mexico City following the devastating earthquake of 1985; the tremors shook up not only the city's buildings but the very legitimacy of the political system and its leadership. As Diane Davis described it in *The Resilient City*, the earthquake exposed a raft of official corruption and abuses—in some cases, quite literally (new government buildings pulverized by the earthquake were found to be of substandard construction quality, and the exposed cellars of ruined police stations contained evidence of torture). These revelations galvanized the capital's "resilient citizens" to demand political accountability and a reordering of reconstruction priorities, including a new focus on low-income housing. It remains to be seen whether New Orleanians will prove as resilient as the people of Mexico City. For one, a scattered populace is very hard to organize politically; the social action that took place in Mexico City is unlikely in New Orleans if a large number of the city's displaced and dispossessed fail to return.

All this underscores the fact that cities are more than the sum of their buildings. A city is a tapestry of human lives and social networks that are essential to the heart and soul of the place. A disaster can tear at this social fabric as terribly as at the physical infrastructure of a city. In New Orleans, this social fabric has long been intimately bonded to the unique geography of the city. The highest ground in New Orleans—the original "Crescent City" formed by the Mississippi's natural levee, including the French Quarter and the Garden District—has long been occupied by the white elite. Blacks lived at the very crest of the natural levee, where they were safe from floods but endured the unpleasant noise and odors of riverfront industry. Creole blacks were concentrated in the triangular Seventh Ward, which begins in the lowlands but comes to a point on the Mississippi levee. "Anglo" African Americans later settled in old "back-of-the-city" neighborhoods, such as Treme, and in the lower reaches of Bywater and the Ninth Ward.

Although there has never been a perfect correlation among elevation, flood risk, race, and class in New Orleans (racially mixed middle-class neighborhoods, such as Lakeview and Pontchartrain Park, built on swampland drained by the Corps of Engineers decades ago, were also badly flooded by Katrina), it most certainly determined who got out of town and who did not. Middle-class whites—and blacks and Latinos and Asians—loaded their SUVs and fled; the poor were stuck without the means or money to find their way to safety. These people have now been scattered to the four winds, in the largest internal migration of Americans since the 1950s. With every passing day, it becomes less and less likely that these and other displaced New Orleanians will ever come home.

If they do not, then the Crescent City's future is dim indeed. A city can be reconstructed without being recovered, and therein lies the great hazard of post-Katrina New Orleans. If history is any guide, there is little doubt this city will be rebuilt in some form. But will New Orleans be recovered as a real and robust metropolis? And whose New Orleans will it be? Recovering a wrecked city involves much more than bricks, mortar, and asphalt—or bits, bytes, and electricity. As we pointed out in *The Resilient City*, it also "fundamentally entails reconnecting severed familial, social and religious networks of survivors. Urban recovery occurs network by network, district by district, not just building by building; it is about reconstructing the myriad social relations embedded in schools, workplaces, childcare arrangements, shops, places of worship, and places of play and recreation."

Public attention will undoubtedly be focused on the rehabilitation of iconic New Orleans—cleaning up Jackson Square and the Vieux Carré, replanting the palm trees on Canal Street, reopening the French Market and the convention center, perhaps building a new Superdome. But aside from scattered arson and looting, the New Orleans of the tourist and entertainment circuit made it through Katrina relatively unscathed. This New Orleans will rebound quickly and vigorously and will even benefit from a surge of "sympathy tourism," much as New York did following 9/11. As Diane Davis put it in her chapter on Mexico City in *The Resilient City*, postdisaster reconstruction follows "a logic of money and power." And in New Orleans, tourism is big money, a backbone of the local economy.

It's altogether another story for the "other" New Orleans, the city far from the beaten tourist track, the city of the Lower Ninth Ward, Treme, and Bywater and other communities inundated by Pontchartrain's floodwaters. The residents of these places may have been poor, but they were an essential part of the Crescent

City's tapestry of cultural life and traditions. They made New Orleans what it was and were as much a part of the soul of the place as were the gracious homes of the Garden District or the Mississippi River itself. Moreover, to take a more pragmatic tack, they were also the folks who cooked and cleaned and served all the tourists and conventioneers that the local economy is so dependent on. If New Orleans is to become again a robust and authentic place, these former residents must be welcomed back and accommodated as enthusiastically as might new corporate investors, real estate developers, or Mardi Gras revelers.

This is not going to be a simple matter. The homes of the dispossessed are likely going to be uninhabitable after stewing in a toxic gumbo for weeks. Block after block of waterlogged structures will need to be bulldozed and sanitized, and it remains to be seen whether the federal government permits any kind of reconstruction in the most flood-prone areas of the city. Making New Orleans home again for all its peoples will be a great challenge. First and foremost it will require building a sophisticated new flood protection infrastructure. It will require building affordable housing, providing job training and placement, improving the public education system, and making a redoubled effort to crush the violent gangs that have made murder a New Orleans specialty. And all this must be done quickly, before the city's displaced residents put permanent roots down elsewhere.

None of this will come cheaply. Should the American people subsidize the immense costs of recovering New Orleans? Should residents of Massachusetts or Montana cough up tax money to house the returnees who lost their homes? The answer should come without hesitation: yes. This is a great American city, and it is the responsibility of both the federal government and the American people to help put it back on its feet. If we can spend billions to rehabilitate Baghdad and Basra, surely we can do the same for one of our own. The stakes are terribly high. If New Orleans is not fully recovered—if little is done to meet the needs of all racial and class backgrounds, if social problems that have long bedeviled the city's poorest communities are not tackled head-on, if reconstruction focuses exclusively on high-profile projects aimed at getting the tourists and conventioneers back and spending—then the city will slip into a kind of glamorous but irrelevant afterlife. It will become what many urbanists fear most—a Crescent City theme park, an island of Fat Tuesday fun with a Starbucks on every corner, insulated by a "clean zone" of bulldozed neighborhoods where once lived the very peoples who gave us jazz and jambalaya and made New Orleans the gritty legend it once was.

THOMAS J. CAMPANELLA

is assistant professor of urban design and city planning at the University of North Carolina at Chapel Hill and a visiting professor at Nanjing University's Graduate School of Architecture. He co-edited *The Resilient City: How Modern Cities Recover from Disaster* (New York: Oxford University Press, 2005) with Lawrence J. Vale of the Massachusetts Institute of Technology.

This article was originally published by Planetizen on September 21, 2005.

THE END OF TALL BUILDINGS

James Howard Kunstler and Nikos A. Salingaros

In their article, written a week after the terrorist attacks of September 11, 2001, the authors declare an end to architecture that reaches for the clouds. This is a move they believe would lead to improved urban centers. Five years later, Nikos Salingaros provides an update to the article in response to the article's original critics.

Our world has changed dramatically.

Watching video of the burning twin towers of the World Trade Center in the few minutes before they both collapsed, we were struck by what appeared to be the whole history of the skyscraper captured in vignette. In the blocks east and south of the World Trade Center stood the earlier skyscrapers of the twentieth century, including some of the most notable prototypes of that epoch. Virtually all of these pre-1930 ultra-tall buildings thrust skyward with towers, turrets, and needles, each singular in its design, as though reaching up to some great spiritual goal as yet unattained. And there, in contrast, stood the two flaming towers of the World Trade Center, with their flat roofs signifying the exhaustion of that century-long aspiration to reach into the heavens, their failure made even more emphatic in the redundancy of their banal twinness. Then they and everything inside them imploded into vapor and dust, including several thousand New Yorkers whose bodies will likely never be found.

The United States was attacked by terrorists on September 11, 2001. With the recent tragedies comes a sobering reassessment of America's (and the world's) infatuation with skyscrapers. We feel very strongly not only that the disaster should be blamed on the terrorist action but that this horrible event exposes an underlying malaise with the built environment.

We are convinced that the age of skyscrapers is at an end. It must now be considered an experimental building typology that has failed. Who will ever again feel safe and comfortable working 110 stories above the ground? Or sixty stories? Or even twenty-seven? We predict that no new megatowers will be built and that existing ones are destined to be dismantled. This will lead to a radical transformation of city centers—which, however, would be an immensely positive step toward improving the quality of urban life. The only megatowers left standing a century hence may be in those developing countries who so avidly imported the bric-a-brac of the industrialized world without realizing the damage they were inflicting on their cities. This essay looks at criticisms of tall buildings while offering some practical solutions.

Tall Buildings Generate Urban Pathologies

In a paper entitled "Theory of the Urban Web," published in 1998 and reprinted in his 2005 *Principles of Urban Structure* (Amsterdam, The Netherlands: Techne Press, 2005), Salingaros outlined structural principles for urban form. The processes that generate the urban web involve nodes, connections, and the principles of hierarchy. Among the theoretical results derived were multiple connectivity—in which a city needs to have alternative connections in order to stay healthy—and the avoidance of overconcentrating nodes. When the second pathology occurs, such as in segregated-use zoning and in monofunctional megatowers, it kills the city by creating a mathematical singularity (where one or more quantities become extremely large or infinite). Many pathologies of contemporary cities are traced to ideas of early Modernist planning that appeared in a totally unrealistic context in the 1920s.

In all cases and to some degree, high-rise buildings deform the quality, the function, and the long-term health of urbanism in general by overloading the infrastructure and the public realm of the streets that contain them. Leon Krier has referred to this as "urban hypertrophy," making the additional point that overloading any given urban center tends to prevent the organic development of new healthy, mixed urban fabric anywhere beyond the center (Leon Krier, *Houses, Palaces, Cities*, New York: St. Martin's Press, 1984). Bear in mind, too, that some of the sturdiest and even aesthetically pleasing tall buildings of the early twentieth century are only now approaching the end of their so-called "design life." What is their destiny?

The worst offender in this urban destruction is the monofunctional megatower. Paradoxically, it has become an icon of modernity and progress—how can images dating from the 1920s be considered modern? Indoctrination at its most subversive has successfully identified the glass and steel boxes of Ludwig Mies van der Rohe with a phony "efficiency." Voices raised against the skyscraper include that of the architect and urbanist Constantine Doxiades (documented by Peter Blake in *Form Follows Fiasco*, London, UK: Little, Brown, 1974, 82):

My greatest crime was the construction of high-rise buildings. The most successful cities of the past were those where people and buildings were in a certain balance with nature. But high-rise buildings work against nature, or, in modern terms, against the environment. High-rise buildings work against man himself, because they isolate him from others, and this isolation is an important factor in the rising crime rate. Children suffer even more because they lose their direct contacts with nature, and with other children. High-rise buildings work against society because they prevent the units of social importance—the family . . . the neighborhood, etc.—from functioning as naturally and as normally as before. High-rise buildings work against networks of transportation, communication, and of utilities, since they lead to higher densities, to overloaded roads, to more extensive water supply systems—and, more importantly, because they form vertical networks which create many additional problems—crime being just one of them.

Peter Blake condemned megatowers in *Form Follows Fiasco* on several points. One was the disastrous wind shear that their surfaces created; the other was fires that had burned out of control in two skyscrapers in Latin America. He warned the world (p. 150) that:

the first alternative to Modern Dogma should obviously be a moratorium on high-rise construction. It is outrageous that towers more than a hundred stories high are being built at a time when no honest engineer and no honest architect, anywhere on earth, can say for certain what these structures will do to the environment—in terms of monumental congestion of services (including roads and mass-transit lines), in terms of wind currents at sidewalk level, in terms of surrounding water tables, in terms of fire hazards, in terms of various sorts of interior traumata, in terms of despoiling the neighborhoods, in terms of visually polluting the skylines of our cities, and in terms of endangering the lives of those within or without, through conceivable structural and related failures.

We just saw two of the tallest buildings in the world burn and implode so that all their construction material (and contents—furniture plus people) was particulated, and the residue compressed into the space of the underground parking garage. All of this happened on the order of minutes. Did no one read Blake's warnings? Certainly many people did, but the persuasive force of the Modernist architectural image of slick, shiny towers going all the way back to Le Corbusier's first drawings in the 1920s was more seductive than practical realities and risks.

As of September 11, 2001, we cannot afford to be so complacent—or so easily entranced by the totems of "modernity." Every would-be terrorist who is now a child will grow up and be instructed by those surreal, riveting images of the two airplanes crashing into the World Trade Towers.

A New Urban Life and Alternatives to Megatowers

The New Urbanism has some (though by no means all) solutions that could reintroduce life into formerly dead urban environments. These ideas go back to several authors, including Christopher Alexander. In his book *A Pattern Language* (New York: Oxford University Press, 1977), Alexander proposed with his co-authors 253 "patterns" that describe how to satisfy human needs in the built environment, from the scale of a city down to the scale of detailed construction in a room. Two of those patterns are relevant to our discussion:

> Pattern 21: FOUR-STORY LIMIT. "There is abundant evidence to show that high buildings make people crazy. Therefore, in any urban area, no matter how dense, keep the majority of buildings four stories high or less. It is possible that certain buildings should exceed this limit, but they should never be buildings for human habitation."

> Pattern 62: HIGH PLACES. "The instinct to climb up to some high place, from which you can look down and survey your world, seems to be a fundamental human instinct. Therefore, build occasional high places as landmarks throughout the city. They can be a natural part of the topography, or towers, or part of the roofs of the highest local building—but, in any case, they should include a physical climb."

We agree that the first of these "patterns" might appear utopian and irrelevant to the industrialized world. However, our purpose is to reexamine the most basic aspects of urbanism and, in particular, to look at those factors that have been destroyed by the megalomania of architects and the speculative greed of builders.

A city requires high buildings, but not all of them should be high, and they should certainly be of mixed use.

It is not possible to state with any certainty exactly what the optimum height of buildings ought to be, since buildings greater than ten stories are an experimental product of industrial technology—itself an experiment for which the results are not yet in. We do know that the center cities of Paris, London, and Rome achieved excellent density and variety with structures under ten stories and have continued to thrive without succumbing to the extreme hypertrophy characteristic in American urbanism.

Within the upper limits of proven traditional type, it might be prudent to confine future constructions to, perhaps, ten-story office buildings whose four bottom stories are strictly residential. Coexisting with the first type might be five-story residential buildings with a commercial ground floor devoted to retail and restaurants. Both of these are a good compromise between traditional typologies, the ideal solutions proposed by Alexander, and the unfortunate, inhuman, alienating extant urbanisms that have been produced by modernist planning.

One of the most pressing commercial questions after the terrorist devastation of lower Manhattan is, where is the financial world going to find several million square feet of office space? The answer: right in front of our noses. Move into and renovate the numerous depressed areas just a few subway stops away. With the proper mixed-zoning legislation needed to protect residents and guarantee a thriving street life, this could mark the rejuvenation of parts of the city that for years have had the same bombed-out appearance as "ground zero" of the Twin Towers has now (except that the slums are not shown on the evening news). Former President Bill Clinton has set a shining example by moving his offices into Harlem.

Should the World Trade Center be rebuilt as a symbol of the defiance of the American people, as some sentimentalists have proposed in the aftermath of their collapse? We think not. If nothing else, it would be a disservice to humanity to rebuild proven death traps. Obsessively returning to the models of yesterday's tomorrow would refute mankind's past architectural achievements—and, curiously, would be a frightening parallel to the dogmatism that led the terrorists to do their mission.

It's the Fault of the Architects

Why are the above solutions, all available for decades now, not implemented to regenerate our cities? Several factors, including zoning, commercial speculation, and the tax structure, created a favorable climate for erecting megatowers. That era is now over. We conclude with a broad indictment of the architectural and building professions as responsible for destroying our cities and for putting people at risk in firetraps from which they can never be evacuated in time.

Charles, the Prince of Wales, spoke out courageously against megatowers and was consequently accused by architects and the media as being "against progress." The reaction was so severe that for a while his succession to the throne was in question. It is worth recalling his remarks, which, through his choice of words, now seem eerily prophetic. In criticizing the then-unbuilt Canary Wharf tower in London, Charles said: "What hope for London now? Cesar Pelli's tower may become the tomb of modernistic dogma. The tragedy is that it will cast its shadow over generations of Londoners who have suffered enough from towers of architectural arrogance" (*A Vision of Britain*, New York: Doubleday, 1989).

Charles's remarks were only one decade too early.

JAMES HOWARD KUNSTLER

is the author of four books: *The Geography of Nowhere* (New York: Simon and Schuster, 1993), *Home from Nowhere* (New York: Simon and Schuster, 1996), *The City in Mind: Notes on the Urban Condition* (New York: Free Press, 2001), and *The Long Emergency* (New York: Atlantic Monthly Press, 2005). He lives in Saratoga Springs, New York.

NIKOS A. SALINGAROS, ICTP,

is a world-respected urbanist and architectural theorist. He is professor of mathematics at the University of Texas at San Antonio and is concurrently on the architecture faculties of the universities of Rome III, Delft, and Querétaro, Mexico. He has written three books: *Principles of Urban Structure* (Amsterdam, Techne Press, 2005), *A Theory of Architecture* (Solingen, Umbau-Verlag, 2006), and *Anti-Architecture and Deconstruction* Solingen, Umbau-Verlag, 2004).

This article was originally published by Planetizen on September 17, 2001.

RESPONSES FROM READERS

The End of Tall Buildings: A Historical Perspective

The conclusion that tall buildings will not be built and that many will be dismantled does not take history into consideration.

Human beings will always forget the past, given enough time. Our culture revolves around us making the same mistakes over and over again.

Many cities are constantly growing with little regard to land and environmental concerns. I am not saying that one single building of one hundred stories is better than a hundred separate one-story buildings, but in areas such as New York, high-rises do save green space. From a planning standpoint, New York is one of the only cities where its downtown is still alive after 5 p.m. That is clearly due to the city's density. Spreading the buildings out will do the opposite of building communities. Use the standard office park in every city of America as an example: they are ghost towns at night and on the weekends, and most everyone commutes to lunch by car.

For a while the skyscraper will be on hold. Not for very long, though.

—September 17, 2001

Empty Speculation from the Theoretical Fringe

There are, I believe, two ways to interpret this irresponsible and rather ridiculous article: (1) the authors are making a desperate attempt to be provocative and thus attract attention to themselves, or (2) the authors are completely removed from the realities of contemporary construction. The reality is probably a little of both.

There is certainly something to be said about how extreme point density reduces the quality of an urban environment. This topic requires an educated debate, however, replete with facts, figures, and research from which to draw rational conclusions. To suppose that a quote from the likes of Leon Krier is enough to prove a valid point is an insult to rigorous intellectual discourse and an insult to the people who read this article.

To further assert that high-rise buildings are deathtraps in light of recent events represents a sad attempt to use a national tragedy to further one's cause. Real facts regarding fires in high-rise buildings must be presented to assert this claim; otherwise, it is completely without merit. Any building subject to the impact of a large jetliner is a deathtrap, and this includes the Pentagon, which was not a high-rise building.

To blame architects for "destroying our cities" is to credit the profession with having more power than it actually does. I assume that the authors' view of reality works something like this:

Client: "We need five hundred thousand square feet, but only want to do an environmentally sound, low-rise building that covers eight city blocks."

Architect: "No, no, you must build a high-rise monument to my ego."

Are we really to believe that people like Donald Trump have been subject to this sort of insidious, anti-urban influence by the "architectural and building professions"? Let me be the first to deliver reality to your doorstep. It's the people with the money who shape the cities. And that's certainly not the architects.

—September 17, 2001

The Failure of Academic Theory

To say the least, the authors seem dated at best. As an architect and a war veteran, I recognize the flaws in both this article and its intent.

Cities are not "created" by planning theories; they are created by processes, which are driven by people. The negative products of these processes are what city planners then work to deal with. Planning strategies that create too much interference with these processes eventually create an environment that is favorable to the culture of said people, thereby destroying the urban environment they aimed to aid. Hence, extreme congestion in cities like New York and San Francisco led to their mass transit system, extreme density has led to high-rises, and extreme population growth in cities like Los Angeles has led to urban sprawl (the proposition of the authors). The problem can then be quantified as "people." If these people would just stop living like they do and live more like the English, the French, or the Italians, then we could build cities like London, Paris, and Rome!

—September 17, 2001

Diminishing the Tragedy by Theoretical Fiat

It was only a matter of time until someone tried to take the World Trade Center tragedy and debase it for his own ends. We just didn't expect the attempt to come so soon—or, for that matter, to be as patently facile as this piece.

First, we take tremendous issue with two writers who would seek to wring support for their side in a theoretical architectural debate from what is arguably the worst human tragedy in American history. Kunstler and Salingaros diminish the magnitude of this tragedy several times in their article for no greater end than rhetorical flourish.

Why should these authors concern themselves with such piddling concerns as the economic pressures and benefits of rebuilding? Or with the geopolitical message sent by dusting off and reemerging? Or with the effects to New York City's tax base of permanently losing so much office space? There is nary an answer to any of these questions in this article.

To argue that the disaster "not only should be blamed on the terrorist action" is foolishness. Of course this event should be solely blamed on the terrorist action. Any "malaise" that arises from this event has very little to do with the "built environment" per se and much more to do with the fact that two airplanes were intentionally crashed into the "built environment," thereby producing an "unbuilt environment." There can be little doubt that Pentagon workers will feel the same apprehension, reluctance, and fear in returning to work that anyone in Chicago's Sears Tower or Boston's Prudential Center or San Francisco's Transamerica Pyramid will feel. Yet those Pentagon workers occupy a building that is as close to completely horizontal as modern architecture has produced.

The truly negative result of these acts and precisely what the terrorists had tried to accomplish was extinguishing the American spirit. How sad it would be if we admitted their victory and began planning our cities, monuments, and buildings on the premise of extreme events!

History would also disagree with these authors. While the authors proclaim the decentralization of cities and the leveling of skylines as a result of this event, one must note that cities have endured tragic events for millennia and have only grown stronger from them. Whether it was the Fire of Rome in 64 A.D., the Great London Fire of 1666, or the Great Chicago Fire of 1871, each caused technological advances and improvements, and the cities marched on. We should examine what can be learned from this tragedy and what technology and materials can be improved. We shouldn't be in the business of dismissing modern urban form in reactionary, breathless, and tendentious articles.   —*September 27, 2001*

Towers Necessary in Many Cities

The "end of tall buildings" prophesied in this article will not occur. If anything, as the world's population continues to increase and land becomes scarcer in many countries, tall buildings will become more of a necessity. Cities such as Tokyo and Hong Kong must build upward for the simple fact that there is insufficient room to spread outward. The incredible amount of office space required for New York City to maintain its status as the world's premier financial center still remains. Even London is finally having to allow more towers in its Central Business District and Canary Wharf areas. What I think we will see, and have been seeing for several years now, is decreased demand for high-rise office space outside those few cities that remain national and international centers for financial and business concentration. In Canada, where I live, there remains a significant demand for office space in the cores of the nation's two biggest financial and head office centers, Toronto and Calgary, but little anywhere else.

The other trend I see continuing is the construction of high-rise residential towers in cities all over the world. Since the September 11 attacks, we have seen projects continue to move forward in Australia that will be among the tallest residential towers in the world. While banks may think twice before financing any buildings eighty or one hundred stories tall (except in many Asian cities where the tremendous densities make it a necessity), I don't think the world will be paralyzed by fear at the thought of living or working in a fifty-story building. The sinking of the *Titanic* did not end the era of ocean liners; in fact we have seen a renaissance of this type of travel in recent years. The September 11 attacks have not ended our reliance on airplanes, nor will they end our reliance on skyscrapers. More likely, they will result in improvements to public safety considerations in the design process. *—January 31, 2002*

The "End" of Tall Buildings

It is with a profound sense of humor I can read the prediction of "The End of Tall Buildings" in the spring of 2005 while working and living in downtown Manhattan. The building replacing the World Trade Center is planned to be the tallest in the world, at 1,776 feet, and in a month I will move into a fifty-second-floor apartment in a new residential tower built nearby on Gold Street. Skyscrapers are what make New York City into New York City instead of an Akron, Ohio, or similar place. And New Yorkers wouldn't have it any other way. In addition, several new buildings across the globe have recently been announced that will vie for the title of the world's tallest. The predictions of the authors were completely wrong as are the assumptions they were founded on. *—April 4, 2005*

AUTHOR'S UPDATE

"The Uninsurable Skyscraper"

The French are again thinking of introducing skyscrapers into Paris, an idea vetoed by previous governments. Mounting commercial pressures, however, supported by enormous money interests and a propaganda campaign from the architectural establishment, cry out for expensive architectural icons. In an interview for the French scientific journal *Sciences et Avenir* (No. 691, September 2004, p. 63), I said that introducing skyscrapers would be "like dropping a bomb on Paris."

Powerful politicians are supporting the erection of skyscrapers—the taller the better—for entirely iconic reasons. Skyscrapers are still the cheap alternative for every country that does not want to spend the money or put in the real effort toward modernization: to improve its infrastructure, education, health care, and political systems. Naturally, architects find here a golden opportunity for vast profit by offering companies, cities, and countries with an inferiority complex a means of achieving status by building the world's tallest building.

While architects were promoting skyscrapers on aesthetic and ideological grounds, the insurance industry moved to make their erection more expensive and less feasible. Champions of skyscrapers have ignored this crucial development. A little-known paper by J. H. Johnson Jr. and J. D. Kasarda ("9/11 Reassessments of Urban Location Costs and Risks," *Real Estate Issues*, Summer 2003, pp. 28–35) presented important developments summarized here:

1. General insurance premiums for business properties have increased from two to ten times after 9/11. Most new policies have a terrorist exclusion provision. This affects new construction, since financing is contingent on full insurance coverage. Companies are forced to self-insure, using up money that was formerly available for business investments and job creation.

2. Even when primary insurance can be covered, there is no backup from re-insurers, who no longer offer terrorism coverage. The U.S. federal government had to step in to replace (but only in part) the role of re-insurers.

3. Increased security for high-rise office buildings has to be borne by the companies, which are responsible for common area maintenance costs. Increased security takes up valuable time in daily access to the building.

4. Firms are quietly relocating away from high-rise targets in metropolitan centers. One reason is that most high-rises are not designed for mass evacuations. The same is true for highly visible public buildings. These added costs are reducing the attractiveness and competitiveness of large cities and metropolitan areas.

5. These effects will begin to be felt only after the end of 2004, when many long-term commercial real estate leases in place in 2001 have expired.

In the face of these hard assessments of the real-estate market, proposing new skyscrapers for cities makes no business sense. Developments such as the insurance and energy situations will eventually halt skyscraper construction.

Monstrous skyscrapers are elements of urban pathology. Nevertheless, I happen to admire the skyscraper typology from its glorious first days at the turn of the twentieth century up to the last relatively modest Art Deco buildings in the 1920s (e.g., the Flatiron Building in New York City and others of its vintage, especially those by skyscraper pioneer Louis Sullivan). These and the later Art Deco buildings are among America's greatest achievements—from ten to twenty stories—with quite a thin footprint and a meticulous attention to promoting life on the ground floor. Their base is integrated as much as possible into the urban fabric.

After that, their size became too large, and their humane design was abandoned for the alien and faceless modernist style. A monster skyscraper relies on a false conception of complexity. Large constructions, such as a petrochemical plant, bring together pieces that necessarily interact (chemical processes and pipes), because those connect with each other to perform a technological and industrial task. Every piece of the petrochemical plant is there to interact with every other piece. The modern skyscraper, by contrast, concentrates non-interacting parts. Offices don't all interact with one another. They interact electronically with people *outside* that building. There's absolutely no reason for all those people to be physically together.

Like a tree with leaves, the skyscraper you see sticking up hides an even bigger invisible "root" system down below. The skyscraper has to be fed with enormous energy and other resources. It's ridiculously expensive and eventually impoverishes the city. The taller the building gets, the more it needs to be supported systemically, so it parasitizes a vast surrounding area. Maintaining a skyscraper in an urban setting is akin to maintaining a space colony. The problem is supply and transportation. Trying to connect to the ground leads to extraordinary problems. There is a future for skyscrapers—as urban prisons. The security is excellent because it is supported by the geometry: vertical isolation and no need to interact with real life on the ground.

Finally, skyscraper architects are offering us the same pie-in-the sky palliatives to the security aspect, trying to distract people's attention with unproven space-age technological gimmicks. A fundamental law of engineering design is to work *with* the geometry, instead of *against* it. Consider the number of stories that a person can feasibly and quickly run downstairs. A comfortable height is around seven stories plus or minus two, a number that comes from cognitive psychology. One can stretch this by a few stories but not by many more.   —*September 2006*

FORTIFYING AMERICA: PLANNING FOR FEAR

Edward J. Blakely |

Published just weeks after the world-changing events of September 11, 2001, this article and readers' comments provide a snapshot of the planning community's attempts to understand recent events and their impact on our built environment. In the article, author Edward J. Blakely calls for professional planners to take a new ethical stand. Predicting the increasing popularity of gated and walled residential complexes among residential real estate developers in the aftermath of the terrorist attacks, Blakely asks planners to consider what kind of security will actually protect citizens rather than divide them.

Franklin D. Roosevelt said, "The only thing we have to fear is fear itself."

We are now a fearful and tearful nation. Our fears are our enemies in many ways. This became very clear after the terrorist attacks on the World Trade Center. But the fear within the nation did not start on September 11, 2001. It started when we as a nation began the process of separating ourselves more deeply by race and class. As we have segregated our communities, we have created wedges of fear across our country. According to the latest U.S. census figures, we are more deeply segregated than at any time since the Civil War. As a segregated, ghettoized nation, we have created fear compounds. Some of these compounds house the rich in gated communities. Others restrain the poor with freeway walls and railroad tracks. The symbols of social and economic distance were in some ways illustrated by the Twin Towers.

As we try to recover from this tragedy, we are finding it hard to find ways to recognize the lives of the poor dishwashers as we mourn the lives of stockbrokers, financiers, and public safety officials. This separate mourning process compounds our tragedy. Already as New York seeks to heal itself, there are voices that protest the notion of rebuilding the segregated social fabric of Wall Street and the deeply segregated New York Fire Department and the equally segregated building trades. We do not need these wedges in our society as we try to bring the nation together; we have to build away from fear, not toward more fear through less socioeconomic balance.

Signs of Fear

The early signs are not good. Fortress mentality is already at work. Most of the news is about arming pilots and adding more police and National Guard at airports and elsewhere. This talk, along with plans for military operations, misses the point. The real war here will not be won by a few smart bombs that we can see on television.

There are increasing moves to seal our borders and reduce immigration as well as increase surveillance on our own citizens. All of this is fear building, which creates a winning atmosphere for our new adversaries. The real battle here is for hearts and heads. We cannot bomb or subdue ideas, particularly when these ideas prey on our own soft underbelly of inequality.

America cannot and should not go down the road of the deeply divided developing world with compounds for the wealthy complete with armed guards, as in nations like Venezuela and Mexico, where high walls and armored cars protect the wealthy from the peasants. If we imitate this form of physical, symbolic segregation, we will end up defeating ourselves from within. This is precisely what our new enemies want.

Planning Against and Not For Fear

As professional planners, we have to take a new ethical stand. We have to ask, what kind of security will protect us and what kind will divide us. Gated and walled residential complexes will be even more popular among residential real estate developers. New forms of separated social institutions will be seen as merely pragmatic, and some forms of racial and ethnic and religious segregation will be considered tolerable. All of these forms of fear-inducing behavior choke the core of democracy and a free society. We who are planners must not give into fear in the form of a little fencing here and a few walls there. Even in its most seemingly benign form, fear-based separation has the seed of destroying an entire nation. Let's not give in, and we win.

was dean of the Robert J. Milano Graduate School in New York City at the time of this article. He is a fellow of the National Academy of Public Administration and was previously dean of the School of Urban Planning and Development at the University of Southern California in Los Angeles. Blakely also served as the chair of city and regional planning at the University of California at Berkeley, where he assisted the City of Oakland recovery efforts from both the earthquake in 1989 and the fires in 1991. He is the author of *Fortress America: Gated Communities in the United States* (Thousand Oaks, CA: Brookings Institution Press, 1997) and the co-author of *Fundamentals of Economic Development Finance* (Sage, 2001). He is now professor of urban planning at the University of Sydney and continues to be engaged in city rebuilding in New Orleans, Asia, and Australia.

This article was originally published by Planetizen on October 2, 2001.

RESPONSES FROM READERS

The Fear Psychology

A true democracy is one where the citizen experiences physical and mental freedom. One of the basic concepts of terrorism is to strike at this level. September 11 will be a blow to the world's greatest democracy not in the form of intelligence failure but as one where the very basis of democracy will be increasingly limited. The biggest challenge for the planner shall be to deal at this proverbial level of planning. Time will tell whether "the fear psychology" holds up or is broken down by holding true to the meaning of democracy.   —*October 2, 2001*

Unacceptable Misuse of the Misery of Others

It's been said many times in the past few weeks that a national tragedy brings out the worst and best in a people. We've seen some of the best in the actions of ordinary people on a hijacked plane. These people recognized that they were doomed but chose to fight against further slaughter. We've also seen average Americans who have stepped out of their daily lives to volunteer to help strangers in any way they could.

Unfortunately, we've also seen those who should have known better try to use this tragedy to forward their own agenda. We've seen supposedly respected commentators in the architectural field suggest that tall buildings cause pathology—that the buildings invited their own doom. And now we see a social commentator connecting segregation in this country to this atrocity, arguing that our natural desire to prevent further harm will result in greater segregation, that a fire department decimated by tragedy should not be rebuilt because it was segregated, and that we mourn only because wealthy people were slaughtered.

Mr. Blakely, this essay is an opportunistic misuse of the misery of others. I can only hope that those persons (of all races, religions, and sexual orientations) whose loved ones perished in this outrage never read your words and feel even more pain. I hope people outside of the field of planning are not reading this material and thinking that planners are this uncaring. You owe those mourners—as well as those who struggle in this country to right the wrongs of segregation—an apology.
                                                                    —*October 4, 2001*

AUTHOR'S RESPONSE

It has been more than five years since the tragic events of September 11, 2001. Readers of this opinion piece offered their own analysis of the situation and the prospects for the nation. One took exception to the notion that America's problems of income and race should be the foci of the narrative on September 11. On reflection, I agree to a point. The data and observations were right, but the essay does take a "blame the victims" tone that was not intended.

Americans have shown remarkable cohesion and tolerance since the tragic events of 9/11 notwithstanding the deep and continuing political and social fragmentation described by several commentators to the essay. The United Kingdom and other nations have found their societies far less able to handle internal debate and dissent. Let's count our blessings. Nonetheless, we cannot lose sight of the need to make sure the American rendezvous with equality remains the nation's primary goal.

Gates, walls, and other signs of fear do divide us socially or politically. There was no intention in the essay to suggest that people should not grieve for one another regardless of status. And the essay pointed to the opportunity to re-build New York on a more equitable basis. Fortunately, many New Yorkers shared my views, and I became a central figure in building a citizen coalition across all races, classes, and orientations to rebuild Lower Manhattan and all of New York City.

This work is not done but we are working together, as I suggested doing it with all voices included. As I said before in the opinion above, the only way any outside force can harm the United States is by us losing sight of the nation's unique mission to ensure freedom and liberty and equality for all of its citizens.

—September 2006

PLANNING FOR POST-DISASTER RECOVERY

Robert B. Olshansky |

The recovery process is fraught with challenges, but planners have the perfect skill set to manage post-disaster reconstruction and ultimately make a difference in a community.

When a disaster strikes—be it earthquake, hurricane, landslide, or explosion—it causes immediate physical effects: lost lives, injuries, damaged homes and businesses, broken infrastructure. We all know that planning is critically needed to mitigate the effects of such disasters. Mitigation tools include development review procedures, siting guidelines, area hazard studies, building codes, engineering structures, public purchase, and strategies to relocate, strengthen, or otherwise modify existing structures.

The moment of destruction, however, is only one part of the disaster. Disasters extend over time. Disasters disrupt lives and businesses, as people await compensation, infrastructure repair, and the return of their neighbors. The physical recovery from disasters takes many years, and the psychological scars can last for decades. Many people survive the initial disaster but then suffer from the recovery, as the economy stagnates, social networks weaken, and health care and support services decline. This is true of all disasters but is currently particularly visible in New Orleans following Hurricane Katrina.

The Common Characteristics of Recovery

Based on experience with many disasters around the world, we can identify many common features of recovery processes. These include the following:

Urban Systems and Physical Change

- Negative trends that existed before the disaster will usually worsen during the recovery period.

- Cities usually rebuild in the same place and with the same general urban form, in all but the most catastrophic of disasters. This is because economic and social networks are more resilient than buildings.

- Cities see physical improvements after disasters. Changes are never as much as planners would like, but some level of incremental improvement always occurs.

- Citizens resist relocation of residential areas, and relocations without citizen support and participation are likely to fail.

Equity

- The higher the socioeconomic level, the more likely households and businesses are to recover to pre-disaster levels. Conversely, those with the fewest resources get less attention from aid organizations and get it later in time.

Outside Resources

- Outside resources—in the form of money, supplies, technical assistance, and employees—are vital. But the money is never enough.

Process

- At a minimum, the goal of recovery is to return to the previous level of economic function and replace the quantity of lost housing units. Beyond that, the recovery process depends on local social and economic context as well as local and national politics.

- Bureaucracies lack the flexibility to be able to quickly respond to the uncertainties of the recovery process. As a result, new community-based organizations emerge. Such organizations are, in fact, crucial to a successful recovery process.

- Government agencies can facilitate recovery to the extent that they can support—financially and technically—local organizations and not tie their hands with excessive requirements. It is important to realize that much of recovery occurs through family and informal networks.

- Citizen participation is essential to help determine recovery goals, provide communication during the recovery process, and ensure community support.

Planning Strategies

- Speed is important in rebuilding. It is important in order to keep businesses alive, rebuild infrastructure, and provide temporary and permanent housing for disaster victims. Even if official agencies do not act quickly, many victims will begin to rebuild on their own—in a manner and location that they determine, even if uncoordinated with services.

- Conversely, taking the time to plan the post-disaster reconstruction is also important. It is important to make this new, permanent city the best it can be. Planning can help coordinate land uses and infrastructure, ensure safety, promote design that will improve the quality of residents' lives, account for the concerns of all citizens, and seek cost-effective solutions. But if it takes too long, it will be ineffective.

- Previously existing plans can help to improve both the speed and quality of post-disaster planning. "Existing plans" means much more than simply land use maps. It means that the community has an active planning process, including well-established community organizations, lines of communication, a variety of planning documents and tools, and some degree of community consensus.

- Information is a valuable resource because it provides the basis for strategic planning decisions. Information systems that include inventories of parcels, structures, and hazards can greatly facilitate the recovery process.

The Role of Planning

Post-disaster recovery provides a moment in which planners can shine. Of all the phases of emergency management, this is the one best suited to the skills of planners and is the one in which planners can best make a difference. Recovery is a microcosm of all the challenges of urban planning—developing land use and economic development strategies to improve lives, acting in the absence of sufficient information, making tradeoffs between deliberation and expediency, navigating local politics, engaging the public, attracting appropriate investors, and identifying funding sources to supplement inadequate local resources. Following disaster, however, the stakes increase, public interest is heightened, and time compresses. On the other hand, additional resources usually become available following disasters. The local planner plays a key role in trying to best use those resources while coping with the added stresses inherent to recovery.

The challenge is this: how can local governments effectively manage post-disaster recovery and reconstruction—meeting the time-sensitive needs of housing and economic recovery while also maximizing the opportunity for community betterment? The reality is that post-disaster planning will involve multiple actors and multiple plans, advancing a variety of reconstruction and financing strategies.

Once a disaster occurs, the best way to improve post-disaster planning processes—for providing both speed and quality—is to emphasize information and communication, and explicitly provide funding for them. High-quality, systematic data collection, information systems, and communication mechanisms would be a good start. Planning agencies also must explicitly recognize the conflicting roles of speed and deliberation. Regular communication between agencies can provide the arenas for deciding the tradeoffs between speed and deliberation in real time. Finally, government needs to be committed to supporting fully inclusive planning processes as soon after the disaster as possible.

Better yet, local governments should plan ahead for disaster recovery. As noted by Jim Schwab in *Planning for Post-disaster Recovery and Reconstruction* (Washington,D.C.: American Planning Association, PAS Report 483/484, 1998), a plan helps to better position a community toward accessing post-disaster funding. Having a plan means that local officials have considered a large range of options and have decided how to use post-disaster funding so as to best further all the planning goals of the community. Plans also help communities save critical time by making their funding requests early in the process.

Communities can also adopt a recovery ordinance, using as a guide the model ordinance prepared by Kenneth Topping in *Planning for Post-disaster Recovery and Reconstruction*. This ordinance should address such issues as a coordinating body, distinguishing between long-term and short-term decisions, temporary regulations that suspend normal rules, criteria for declaring moratoria, reconstruction of nonconforming uses, and high-priority mitigation actions.

Finally, disasters are one of the most persuasive arguments for urban planning in general. Communities that have active planning processes—including well-established community organizations, lines of communication, a variety of planning documents and tools, and some degree of community consensus—will recover faster and better than those that do not. Communities that plan are those that are best equipped to deal with unexpected events in general (see *Planning for the*

Unexpected, Laurie Johnson et al., Washington, D.C., American Planning Association, PAS Report 531, 2005).

The Federal Role

The federal government both helps and complicates local recovery planning. Federal funding and resources for infrastructure, temporary and permanent housing, and economic recovery are essential prerequisites for successful recovery. But often the rules are too restrictive to allow local governments to design solutions appropriate to their needs. For example, some funds are most readily available during the first six months, but the needs are often not clear until later on. Such situations demand flexibility to renegotiate terms. Conversely, the Federal Emergency Management Agency's (FEMA's) public assistance program, which reimburses (eventually) public entities for damages caused by the disaster, is notoriously slow and bureaucratic, as FEMA staffers carefully consider the true value of each rusty pipe section prior to the event.

Recently, FEMA has decided to enter the business of post-disaster recovery planning. This initiative toward long-term interdisciplinary thinking is a positive step for FEMA, but it is not clear whether FEMA is well-equipped to operate in the realm of urban planning. This process, bureaucratically numbered ESF-14 ("emergency support function 14") was recently rolled out in the wake of Hurricane Katrina after successful tests in several small communities the previous year. In this process, FEMA pulls together expertise from federal agencies and local expertise to (1) assess local needs, (2) develop plans and projects for recovery funding, and (3) match the local projects with federal funding sources.

Recent experience following Katrina, however, shows that this process does not work well after large disasters or in large urban areas. FEMA is not an agency suited to thinking about long-term planning, and perhaps the U.S. Department of Housing and Urban Development should be considered as an alternative. Better yet, the Stafford Act—the nation's disaster law—should be amended to enable federal funding to directly support local planning activities, beginning immediately after the disaster. Planning funds should be used locally, by state and local agencies and consultants of their choosing.

Recovery is complicated, confusing, and contentious, and it sets the framework that will affect a community for years to come. In short, it is the perfect environment for planning skills. Following disasters, planning is vital, in order to best manage the reconstruction decisions, economic development initiatives, and prioritization of outside funding. In particular, post-disaster planning requires information systems, open processes, and considerable citizen involvement. Before disasters occur, communities should plan ahead for recovery, including adoption of a recovery ordinance. Moreover, good urban planning processes alone can make it much easier to cope with disasters when they occur. Finally, planners need to thank the federal government for its newfound interest in disaster recovery but also ask that these efforts be funded at the state and local levels, where they best belong.

ROBERT B. OLSHANSKY

is professor of urban and regional planning at the University of Illinois at Urbana-Champaign. His teaching and research cover land use and environmental planning, with an emphasis on planning for natural hazards.

SOCIETY AND PLANNING
Introduction by the Editors of Planetizen

Cities are a product of the progression of human societies into complex civilizations and are shaped and molded by the values and aspirations of the societies in which they exist. The café culture of Paris is manifest in its street cafés. Shanghai's ambition is reflected in its ever-sprouting skyscrapers. And no one questions that there is a special attachment to the automobile in Los Angeles.

However, the intimate relationship between cities and society also raises the following questions: What impact does the design and building of cities have on society itself? Could it be that urban planning is an exercise not only in city building but also in social construction?

The past shows examples of planners and builders less than timid about assuming the role of social crusader. The father of the Garden City movement of the early twentieth century, Ebenezer Howard, hoped that his plans for cities—which combined the best of urban and rural life—would lead to more harmonious societies. Indeed, the suburbanization of American cities during the post WWII era partially stems from an American cultural bias toward viewing cities as corrupting influence for society. In the American mind-set, the countryside is virtuous.

Ironically, today it is the suburbs that are increasingly perceived as the corrupting force on our cities. Opponents of urban sprawl decry its profligate use of land, its voracious appetite for energy and resources, and the social isolation and corpulence it engenders in its residents. As more evidence mounts about the environmental, economic, and social costs of conventional suburban development, communities are increasingly eager to model new development on smart growth and New Urbanist principles.

However, a major stumbling block exists in many communities that inhibits such changes from occurring. In countless communities across America, prevailing zoning laws and building codes make it impossible to build the type of dense, compact, neighborhoods that many planners envision. To remedy the problem, a wave of zoning reform is sweeping the country, with designers and developers rallying to change the way we build our cities.

But a funny thing happened on the way to the zoning hearing. In seeking to remove regulatory barriers, advocates for smart growth and New Urbanism have found themselves reluctant allies with another group that traditionally lobbies for a freer regulatory environment: Libertarians. While many smart growth advocates admittedly seek to replace society's old rules forbidding mixed uses and narrow streets with new ones that outlaw one-acre zoning and McMansions, some leaders in the New Urbanism movement favor a different approach. They are increasingly confident, based on the real estate success of existing New Urbanist developments, that in an urban landscape free of proscriptive land use regulations, the market will show that New Urbanist developments are more popular than, or at least competitive with, conventional suburban developments.

The market success of smart growth and New Urbanism has also unleashed a debate about society's responsibility to those farther down the economic ladder. As cities have resurrected their urban cores, real estate prices have surged, displacing an increasing number of low-income inner-city residents. Atlanta, New York, Chicago, and Washington, D.C., are just some of the cities currently grappling with the consequences of their successful urban renaissances.

The impact of economic and market forces has not limited itself to residential real estate. Just as retail outlets have moved toward the big box model to take advantage of economies of scale, so too have our schools. In the arena of public education, the trend of building bigger campuses has provided school districts an opportunity to save money by creating one big box school that more students attend rather than a group of smaller, more local schoolhouses. Yet there is growing recognition that these smaller, neighborhood-oriented schools may provide a higher-quality learning environment along with a better urban environment.

The intersection of planning and law has been an especially controversial topic in recent years—particularly over the issue of eminent domain. While government has the constitutional right to acquire blighted private property for projects deemed of public benefit, the use of this power and what constitutes "blight" and "public benefit" continues to be questioned. The recent U.S. Supreme Court decision in the case of *Kelo v. City of New London*, which ruled in favor of the City of New London, Connecticut, in their taking of private property for a private development, has been a lightning rod for the private property rights movement. The case has sparked a wave of new initiatives and laws across the country seeking to rein in the power of government to acquire or even regulate private land.

All of these new developments show that the role of the urban planner is continually being reshaped. As we learn more about the impact of urban planning on our society, it is beholden on those entrusted with shaping our cities to have a more comprehensive understanding of the full effects of their plans and proposals.

IS GENTRIFICATION REALLY A THREAT?

John Norquist

Should the social virtues of urbanism and new investment in cities get washed out in the hue and cry over "gentrification?" John Norquist, president of the Congress for the New Urbanism, examines the viability of inner-city development trends.

Cities in America have always had an image problem, mostly because they're continually associated with problems. If it's not one thing, it's another. Thomas Jefferson held up the agrarian ideal as preferable to urban life (Why shouldn't everyone live on a plantation with a thousand slaves like he did?). Cities were associated with disease, crime, poverty, sin, and degradation by such reformers as Jacob Riis, Jane Addams, and evangelist Billy Sunday. After World War II, fueled by pro-sprawl housing and highway programs, cities declined. Urban race riots made the decline even more apparent ("Will the last one to leave please turn out the lights?"). Even as late as 1991, when its murder rate peaked, New York City's real estate market and population looked as if they might be on the way down. Thus late-twentieth-century urban policy focused on strategies to attract people and capital back to cities. When signs of revitalization appeared in the strongest of the big cities—New York, Chicago, San Francisco—the policy focus adjusted to include concern for a new problem: displacement of the urban poor by the affluent.

With urban living regaining popularity, reinvestment has spread to some of the smaller markets, as has the concern about displacement or gentrification. Actually, the concern about gentrification seems to be spreading even faster than real estate price appreciation. For example, it has spread to midsized Midwest cities—such as Cleveland, Cincinnati, and Pittsburgh—that went decades with little private sector investment in new housing construction. While this market failure has many legitimate explanations, including redlining and racism, the fact was that demand to live in these cities was low. People, particularly middle-class and affluent whites, were fleeing the city to the suburbs. Rents and sale prices declined or stagnated, and when rents decline, investment shifts to other places. This was doubly bad for the poor. A deteriorating real estate market meant little investment in repair and maintenance of old urban housing stock and, thus, declining housing quality. It also meant the decline and abandonment of the jobs base, tax base, and retail and service structure that had served the departed middle class. Furthermore, because the homogenous, low-density sub-urban development typically allows little, if any, affordable housing, the poor could not easily follow the flight to the suburbs. The only measurable advantage from sprawl for those left behind in the city is low rent.

When consumer demand returns to an urban market, costs and benefits compete for peoples' attention. Bad news: rents will rise. Good news: jobs, tax base, economic structure, and investment return. People, no doubt, would love to pay low rent and experience neighborhood economic prosperity at the same time, but this is difficult unless others subsidize rising rent payments.

In cities with warm but not quite red-hot housing markets, new housing replaces some of that lost to disinvestment, and rents rise slowly, along with such benefits as neighborhood safety, improved transit service, and less time spent traveling to work or stores. In places where rents are stagnant, the discussion of gentrification can lead to government remedies for problems that don't exist yet and may actually chill development as regulatory burdens are layered on prospective projects.

One hopeful characteristic of successful urban redevelopment is that, by its nature, it commonly includes a wider variety of housing types at a wider spread of price points than sprawl. Less-pricey units can be placed in the same building or on the same block with expensive dwellings. For example, people with impressive views pay more than those in units facing the alley. Unlike sprawl, urban infill and rehabilitation at least offer the possibility of people of various incomes living in close proximity.

The social virtues of urbanism and the cost-benefit discussion of new investment in cities tend to get washed out in the hue and cry over "gentrification" when some local activists, community development councils, and armchair liberals assume the heroic mantle of protectors of the poor. While their outrage at urban developers is no doubt self-gratifying, it presents the existing residents of urban neighborhoods a very distorted picture of the costs and benefits of potential redevelopment. If allowed to decide for themselves, low-income people might choose to divert some of their scarce income to paying higher rents and thus take advantage of the benefits of living in improving neighborhoods. In fact, research by Lance Freeman, a Columbia University professor of urban planning, found that low-income residents were no more likely to move from gentrifying neighborhoods than those not experiencing gentrification. As reported in his recent book, he found that many people valued other benefits more than low rents, such as lower crime and restored amenities like shopping or better access to jobs (*There Goes The 'Hood: Views of Gentrification from the Ground Up*, Philadelphia: Temple University Press, August 2006).

Of course, other factors besides renewed investment in cities have left poor and lower-middle-class people struggling. Their payroll taxes have gone up over the past twenty-five years while federal taxes on the rich have dropped, leaving working Americans to shoulder more of the burden. The globalization of the manufacturing sector has forced workers to seek other types of employment, some of it at lower wages. While interest rates remain low, a housing bubble limits the home ownership opportunities of the working poor. At a 2005 summit hosted by the Congress for the New Urbanism at Wingspread in Wisconsin, housing experts from across the political spectrum explored a number of promising policy responses—including making urban neighborhoods with diverse housing stock legal in more communities and replacing inefficient housing programs with an expanded earned-income tax credit that would help low- and moderate-income people earn extra money and spend it on their own priorities (perhaps housing, perhaps not). It's understandable that those in the housing business would want government money devoted to housing, but if ending poverty is the goal, it's good to remember that what low-income people ultimately need to escape poverty is more income.

Against this larger backdrop, the gentrification issue is best understood as nuanced with costs and benefits. It's also better understood in local context—that is, it is genuinely a debatable issue in San Francisco or Manhattan but a totally phony issue in Detroit or Buffalo. Some places fall in the middle of the spectrum. Faint signs of gentrification can be detected in Baltimore, Philadelphia, Milwaukee, and Memphis, but there is so little of it that concern about it should logically be among the lowest priorities. Yet it isn't. The hot rhetoric spewed (perhaps appropriately) in San Francisco gets mindlessly repeated in cities that desperately need investment in their building stock.

Second, even if gentrification happens with little or no concern for the poor, it will in the long run be much better for the low-income population of a metro area than sprawl. The poor have more opportunity in metro areas with compact and economically healthy urban cores. You want the money in the middle, where the poor have a better crack at getting some of it. Example: A poor person in Yonkers is a twenty-five-minute ride from Grand Central and one of the densest job markets on earth. A poor person at 6 Mile and Woodward in Detroit can reach 8 Mile Road by an infrequent bus where the Detroit bus system ends and then catch an even more infrequent bus or van to a far-flung suburban manufacturing or office pod. (Let's say it takes two hours each way, and that would be fast.) My point is that the gentry threat is grossly exaggerated in all but a few megametros and that the obsession with the perceived threat from the moneyed class slows needed reinvestment in most large U.S. cities.

JOHN NORQUIST

is the former mayor of Milwaukee and the author of the book *The Wealth of Cities* (Reading, MA: Perseus Books, 1998). He also serves as president of the Congress for the New Urbanism, which hosts an annual Congress.

This article was originally published by Planetizen on June 6, 2005.

RESPONSES FROM READERS

Different Type of Gentrification

I've read several discussions on who benefits and who suffers when a neighborhood gentrifies. Residential gentrification, it seems, can take two basic forms: renovation of single-family houses and renovation of multifamily buildings. When I think of gentrification, it is the former I think of—I don't know the extent of the latter. The latter, presumably, would displace a lot of low-income people as their building is renovated or replaced. In the case of single-family house gentrification, some of the existing low-income people there would rent and some would own. We've seen evidence that renter turnover during gentrification is less than we thought.

What of the owners? For a neighborhood to gentrify, the houses must turn over from lower-income to higher-income owners because of the investment in buildings required to meet the definition of gentrification. The low-income owners then presumably benefit from higher prices when they sell. If a low-income owner buys in when the prices are low, then acts to improve the house and perhaps the neighborhood through neighborhood involvement, and then sells out when the price goes up, that buyer is the beneficiary of a transfer of wealth from a higher-income buyer. I haven't seen any attempt to study how much this occurs, and it probably varies a lot from city to city, but any attempt to study gentrification should include a study of this. A successful attempt to thwart gentrification may well close off this avenue of wealth creation for lower-income households, thereby sacrificing the interests of some low-income households for the perceived interest of other low-income households.   *—June 6, 2005*

Gentrification *Is* an Issue in Detroit

I do not appreciate the casual approach you take to gentrification in Detroit. Gentrification is an issue for low- and moderate-income residents in Detroit. I suggest you come to a city council hearing for an apartment building that is about to be converted to condominiums and listen to the comments of residents.

Detroit faces many affordable housing issues. Arguably the most challenging is the low median-household income. In many cases, housing cannot be built cheap enough for the "poor people." Further displacing them by converting affordable, quality apartments to condominiums only worsens the problem.

In the past, the city has also attempted to use the power of eminent domain for new housing developments. The result has been the displacement of longtime city residents and home owners for new residential development.

When you examine the number of vacant parcels in Detroit (of which approximately thirty-eight thousand are city owned), it is clear that there is plenty of land to build new, unsubsidized housing. In that sense, gentrification is definitely not a problem. The problem comes in the form of the displacement of existing residents from their affordable dwellings. Many households in Detroit struggle to pay their rents and mortgages—30 percent of all households pay more than one-third of their gross income for housing. These low- and moderate-income households do not have many options. It is important to preserve (and increase) the number of affordable units.

The challenge is to manage gentrification without displacement. Higher-income residents have the potential to bring substantial resources to Detroit (assuming they are moving in from outside the city; contrary to your article, there are affluent Detroiters). Lower-income residents can benefit through increased job opportunities, rising property values, improved schools, additional retail, and stronger institutions.

It is the challenge for planners and housing activists to advocate for solutions that enable a variety of income levels to flourish. Why would you want gentrification to occur with "little or no concern for the poor"? There is plenty of available land in Detroit. It is possible to disentangle gentrification and residential displacement. It isn't necessary to marginalize lower-income residents in favor of gentrification. Doing so only exacerbates problems. A more careful approach will lead to better outcomes for all.

As a final point, the housing market in Detroit has shown signs of improvement recently. In 2003, 5,488 permits were issued for home repair. This accounted for an estimated $59,227,548 in investment. In comparison, there were 735 demolitions in 2003. The cost data are not available for demolitions, but the cost is clearly less than $59 million. Furthermore, new construction in Detroit has increased in recent years. For the past two years, Detroit has had the third most new construction starts in the seven-county metropolitan region.

—June 13, 2005

GENTRIFICATION REALITY TOUR: NEITHER BENIGN NOR BENEVOLENT

Charles Shaw |

To claim that the threat of gentrification is "grossly exaggerated" belies a fundamental misunderstanding of the real threat, the real victims, and the real consequences of inner-city redevelopment, writes Charles Shaw in a passionate response to John Norquist's essay "Is Gentrification Really a Threat?" (Chapter 5.1).

John Norquist, the president of the Congress for the New Urbanism, writes that the threat of gentrification "is grossly exaggerated in all but a few megametros and that the obsession with the perceived threat from the moneyed class slows needed reinvestment in most large U.S. cities."

He also quotes a dubious study by Columbia University professor Lance Freeman that claims that "low-income residents [are] no more likely to move from gentrifying neighborhoods than those not experiencing gentrification."

The poor do not have a choice in the matter. They are being forced out of their neighborhoods, often by much more dire and sinister means than just escalating rents. The North Philadelphia neighborhood of Kensington, one of the nation's poorest and most neglected neighborhoods, exemplifies this problem, as shown in *Drug War Reality Tour*, a documentary by the Sundance Award-winning *Guerrilla News Network* (2003).

Deindustrialization, accompanied by an increase in unemployment, created large ghettos in Philadelphia and other inner cities and some of their adjacent suburbs. The illicit drug market, as well as the rural prison-industrial complex that exploded in the subsequent twenty years as a result of the consolidation of independent farming into big agribusiness, became replacement economies for labor forces that were deemed expendable. As cities began to thrive again in the 1990s, these ghettos became large areas of highly valuable real estate for prospective development. Now, the only problem was how to remove the *Drug*

War Reality Tour, which transports busloads of people into Kensington to witness firsthand the battlefield of America's own domestic Drug War. Throughout the tour, the streetwise members of the Kensington Welfare Rights Union (KWRU) explain the ins and outs of the inner city narco culture and how forces like police complicity and corporate investment are aiding and using the drug epidemic to drive Kensington's people out of their own neighborhood in order to make room for new urban development.

"It's clear that there are forces at play that are using the consequences and devastation of the drug epidemic, and the deterioration of economic conditions, to begin to create a situation where they can push the poor out of urban areas to try to attract the so-called 'Creative Class'—the educated class with the higher incomes—into the inner cities to try and create an infrastructure that will attract investment," says Willie Baptist, education director of the KWRU. "So what you see now is an *acceleration* of this pushing of the poor into the periphery."

Because of the property seizure laws enacted during the last three presidential administrations, the so-called "War on Drugs" has been used to evict tenants and seize inner-city property, which is then auctioned off or sold to waiting developers friendly with the police and city government for barely a fraction of what it is worth. This practice in part helps keep afloat the artificial real estate bubble, which has been keeping the American economy from collapsing in on itself as a result of unemployment, crushing debt, and trade deficits.

In Chicago and New York, two of the most heavily gentrified cities in the nation, promises to rebuild failed public housing and decayed neighborhoods with New Urbanist mixed-income developments have mostly been a Chimera. In Chicago, the Drug War has long been an established apparatus of gentrification, because police flood developing neighborhoods with an occupation-like finality, often making mass arrests of young black and Latino youth under illegal permutations of the controversial "gang loitering ordinance," which prohibits more than four people from congregating together on any given block. Despite the ordinance being struck down by the Illinois Supreme Court, it is still being unofficially enforced, but only when the four or more people in question are young men of color; four white people in the same situation don't even merit a second glance from police. Despite the blatant unconstitutionality of this law and its inherent racial profiling, the message is clear: *things are changing around here, and you are no longer welcome.*

There is no policy apparatus to mandate—nor any incentive to motivate—developers to set aside units for low- to moderate-income families. And when "low-income" units are set aside in Chicago, they are generally for those with an income of $30,000 a year; yet most low-income families make only $8,000 to $12,000 a year, which is barely enough to survive, let alone afford "low-income" housing. Former Chicago Housing Authority residents who wanted to continue living in subsidized housing under the Section 8 voucher program, or move into one of the paltry few replacement units that have been built, have had to undergo Draconian scrutiny as part of screening processes, and very few have been approved. And even if residents do manage to secure Section 8 vouchers, very few private landlords will accept voucher holders as tenants.

Thus continued racism, fear of the poor, and the specter of "drug crime" have given major cities all the pretext they need to forcibly change demographics, displacing hundreds of thousands of poor people—mostly black and Latino minorities. Those displaced are forced to move to the few compact, decaying ghettos that remain (for as long as they remain before they are gentrified) or, increasingly, to decrepit inner-ring suburbs, which are fast becoming the most dangerous places in the nation. And, of course, many remain homeless and living in the streets.

Regarding diminishing tax bases and the need for investment, Norquist posits a monolithic understanding of "investment" by insinuating that the only form available is through the redevelopment of residential real estate. Although redlining and white flight moved most of the middle class out of the industrial cities, there is more than enough money in the wealthy class and the corporate tax base to rebuild our cities a dozen times over. But our government—federal, state, and municipal—has an entrenched policy of profligate corporate welfare, and the George W. Bush tax cuts to the wealthy have had an almost universally deleterious effect on state and municipal budgets across the nation. Despite the budget crises, cities have systematically eschewed taxing corporations, instead giving them tax abatements to beat the band. While corporations more and more are becoming the sole owners of urban real estate, the solution for most city and county governments is to over tax the working-class residents to compensate. This is a massive policy failure that speaks more to the corruption and prevailing robber baron mentality of our so-called leaders and the corporate establishment than it does to population demographics.

How many billions of tax dollars were bilked from urban residents to build private sports arenas in the past twenty years? Or to allow billion-dollar transnationals to erect corporate headquarters in gleaming skyscrapers or introduce big box retail outlets in former residential areas? Yes, cities do need more residents of all sorts, but they are not getting them; what they are getting is a two-class system of the affluent and the desperate-to-indigent, many of whom are there only to work in service jobs for the moneyed classes.

All of this has created what I would characterize as an unspoken, "nudge-nudge, wink-wink" policy to redraw our cities into two-class city-states. Cities, corporations, developers, the "creative class," policy wonks, and apologists hide their intentions behind code words like *market force*, *investment*, and *crime prevention*, when in fact the market system benefits only those with enough capital to dominate it. In addition, "crime issue" has become a code phrase for racism and fear of the poor, as most property and violent crime have significantly receded in the past fifteen years and drug arrests have skyrocketed, in some places by as much as 1,000 percent.

CHARLES SHAW

is a writer and activist living in Chicago. He is editor-in-chief of *Conscious Choice*, senior staff writer and development editor for *The Next American City*, and a regular contributor to *Alternet, Grist, In These Times, Scoop,* and the *Guerrilla News Network*.

This article was originally published by Planetizen on June 14, 2005

RESPONSES FROM READERS

Improvement Is *Not* Inevitable

I can speak only from my own personal experience, and that is this: without gentrification, the decline is continuous and devastating. People in my beloved city (Cincinnati) are dying, in part because activists have deterred urban improvement with the same vehemence that Shaw exhibits. My experience is that there are many, many more urban areas in this country that share the problems of Detroit (flight) than those that suffer from high rents and too much police enforcement. Gentrification is not inevitable, and I know because I see the crime, poverty, and deterioration every day.   *—June 14, 2005*

The Middle Class Has the *Same* Rights as the Poor

The anti-loitering law was struck down several years ago. An educated urbanist such as Mr. Shaw knows this, making it baldly obvious he is just rabble-rousing. Speaking as a member of the "creative class" Shaw refers to, I have as much right to live in any neighborhood I choose as does a person of lesser means. It's not my fault someone else's income is lower than mine.

Just as a Section 8 resident might not be made to feel welcome in the new Trump condo here in Chicago, I certainly am not going to move on down to Englewood either. The urban poor do not have the license on neighborhood accessibility. This whole idea that gentrification is a bad thing is utter nonsense. If I choose to spend my money on housing and sundries elsewhere, who loses out? Not me. The local tax base does. That's no help to the urban poor.   —*June 14, 2005*

If Not Gentrification, What Should Be Done Then?

While I generally disagree with the entire premise of this article, I'm curious which actual policies the author is advocating.

Would it not be beneficial for these residents to try to be a part of the gentrification? What exactly are you doing that would benefit them? How does defending their lives as professional gang members and drug dealers or users benefit them? It seems to me that their path to "progress" (depending on how one defines it) is to participate in gentrification, not prevent it.

Of course, I agree to some degree that some cities go overboard in corporate welfare like gentrification, but that is more a criticism of those particular cities, not of the phenomenon in general.

In perspective, I think it's fair to say that some, even many, gentrification advocates are well intentioned. Can we say the same thing about the gang members and drug dealers whom you describe as victims?   —*June, 15 2005*

AUTHOR'S RESPONSE

It is clear that this is an incendiary issue, and I am happy I was able to throw a little proverbial fuel on the fire.

I do not expect many to agree with me or with my assessments or approach (although, at times, I am not that pleased with it either). It involves challenging too many personal interests of this society of planning and development people.

My intention was not to write something that would be palatable; my intention was to raise awareness about the negative consequences of gentrification and to make unmade connections.

Sometimes, in desperate situations, polite and politically correct language becomes antithetical. This is a dire situation in our cities, no matter the relative scale from city to city or the nation at large. Fundamentally, the academic arguments underlying gentrification (beginning with acknowledging that the official definition of *gentrification* is "the restoration and upgrading of deteriorated urban property by middle-class or affluent people, often resulting in displacement of lower-income people") are deeply socioeconomical, and hence political, in both origin and nature. Moreover, they are being used as justification for related policies that are a legitimate threat to our freedoms. It may be difficult for many to see that now, but persistence will show it eventually.

My personal foibles aside, please do not make the mistake of interpreting this as self-righteousness. There is culpability all around, and I am more than aware of mine. The psychological processes behind racism and—by extension and present association—fear of the poor are so complex and so ingrained into our minute-by-minute thought patterns that it often prevents us from seeing things the way they are or, when seeing it, justifying it through an array of means that often involves dehumanizing some group, such as referring to gang youth as "feral." The term *feral* is defined as "existing in a wild or untamed state, or having returned to an untamed state from domestication." This is precisely the point I have been making. To view another human being as a lesser species that needs to be "domesticated" was the prevailing belief and practice during slavery and colonialism. Enough said about that; the only way to solve the problem is to be empathetic and understanding of the situations that force people into these situations. To think otherwise, in my opinion, is to succumb to the demagoguery of "good" and "evil."

I believe that to be critical thinkers we need to strive to be apolitical humanists, and to be very self-critical of ourselves as a species. This does not make one popular. But it is as necessary to the overall debate as the choir singing the praises.

There is much to learn, but as I discover every day, there is an equal, if not greater, amount to unlearn. We are in the midst of an epidemic of cognitive dissonance in this society. I believe in my heart this is at the root of so much of the animosity that exists these days, including the present situation.

—June 16, 2005

IS *KELO* GOOD FOR URBAN PLANNING?

Samuel R. Staley

A 2005 ruling by the U.S. Supreme Court to uphold the use of eminent domain was seen as an endorsement of professional planning. However, according to Samuel R. Staley, this is not true. The Court's decision upheld the process of eminent domain — but it is not good planning.

When the U.S. Supreme Court announces a decision as important as *Kelo v. City of New London* (545 U.S. 469 [2005]), we often tend to exaggerate its significance. Urban planners can also fall prey to this natural human error.

In *Kelo*, a 5–4 majority upheld the efforts of the City of New London, Connecticut, to redevelop the Fort Trumbull neighborhood. Several home owners and longtime businesses were resisting the city's efforts, arguing that their land was not necessary to achieve the city's goals and that it was not fair to force them from their homes and transfer their land to private developers. The Court disagreed, saying that their property rights were not as important as the city's economic development objectives.

One critical part of the decision leapt out to urban planners and, at first glance, was a ringing endorsement of their livelihood. "Given the comprehensive character of the plan," wrote Justice John Paul Stevens for the majority, "the thorough deliberation that preceded its adoption, and the limited scope of our review, it is appropriate for us, as it was in *Berman [v. Parker]*, to resolve the challenges of individual owners, not on the piecemeal basis, but rather in light of the entire plan. Because the plan unquestionably serves a public purpose, the takings challenged here satisfy the public use requirement of the Fifth Amendment."

The American Planning Association (APA) seized the moment, issuing a press release lauding the decision and likely echoing the sentiments of many in the professional planning community. "The court upholds the use of eminent domain as a vital community tool, as advocated by APA and others concerned with the case," the planners' professional organization declared on June 23, 2005.

"The decision validates the essential role of planning in ensuring fairness in the eminent domain process."

This is not quite true, however. The Court clearly upheld the use of eminent domain for economic development purposes, but to interpret this as support for planning would be a mistake. In fact, all of the Court's references to planning were procedural. No attempt was made to examine the substance of the process or the plan. Whether planning created good or bad outcomes was immaterial.

Indeed, the Court viewed the planning process as little more than open deliberation on economic development policy. On the ground, particularly in cities facing economic decline, local planning commonly becomes the procedural framework in which purely political decisions are made. They often bear little resemblance to planning as most professionals practice it or as students learn about it in their planning courses.

In New London, the "planning process" was really focused on creating jobs and investment. The city attorneys were quite open about both their intent and their purpose: to increase the tax base, create jobs, and generate tax revenues. The objective of the city was not good planning.

A legal planning process does not by itself make for good planning. It does, particularly now, provide a framework in which a broader range of political objectives can be achieved. In *Kelo*, the Court made the leap that an open decision-making process produced fair outcomes and protected the interests of property owners.

Justice Anthony Kennedy's concurring opinion is more salient in this context. "This taking," he wrote, "occurred in the context of a comprehensive development plan meant to address a serious city-wide depression. The city complied with elaborate procedural requirements that facilitate review of the record and inquiry into the city's purposes."

This logic turns the entire concept of civil liberties underlying the U.S. Constitution on its head. The Fifth Amendment, like the other provisions in the Bill of Rights, was intended to provide broad protections. The rights to free speech, a free press, trial by jury, and due process were not intended to be privileges granted by political majorities. The Founding Fathers believed such broad protections guard the rights of minorities against the oppression of the majority and were fundamental to an effective democracy.

To illustrate *Kelo*'s potential damage, recall that its precedent, *Berman v. Parker* (348 U.S. 26 [1954]), substantially relaxed constraints on takings of private property, unleashing a wave of urban renewal that cleared large swaths of

America's cities in the late twentieth century. The results, as even many planners now believe, were devastating for communities. Many areas cleared for urban renewal were never redeveloped, and affordable housing and many potentially vibrant neighborhoods were bulldozed. Not surprisingly, critics now refer to urban renewal as "slum removal," and cynics refer to this period as "Negro removal." The Court's reasoning in *Kelo* grants cities and public officials even broader powers to clear neighborhoods and force families from homes and businesses than those powers granted in *Berman*.

Some have correctly noted that *Kelo* may not change policy. The Supreme Court merely gave a rubber stamp on efforts that have been under way for two decades in the wake of *Poletown Neighborhood Council v. City of Detroit* (304 N.W.2d 455 [Mich. 1981]), which devastated that ethnic community in favor of a General Motors plant. *Poletown* was reversed in August 2004 by the Michigan Supreme Court, but its effect, unlike the original case, is unlikely to be felt far beyond Michigan, given the decision in *Kelo*.

The stakes are higher now than ever before for planners to ensure an open public process and to protect the interests of home owners, businesses, and neighborhoods. Property owners can no longer rely on the federal courts when their property is seized, even when the primary beneficiary will be other private parties. The need for public vigilance in the planning process has been raised to new levels. Without judicial or statutory protections for property rights, planners may be the only ones in the redevelopment process either willing or able to protect the civil liberties of home owners, businesses, and neighborhoods.

SAMUEL R. STALEY,

directs urban and land use policy at Reason Foundation (a nonprofit think tank based in Los Angeles), teaches urban economics at the University of Dayton, and is former chair of his local planning board (in Bellbrook, Ohio). He has written more than one hundred articles, reports, and studies on urban policy and planning. His most recent books include *The Road More Traveled: Why the Congestion Crisis Matters More Than You Think and What We Can Do About It* (New York: Rowman and Littlefield, 2006) and *Smarter Growth: Market-based Strategies for Land-use Planning in the 21st Century* (Westport, CT: Greenwood Press, 2001).

This article was originally published by Planetizen on July 5, 2005.

RESPONSES FROM READERS

Eminent Domain: More Pain than Gain?

While I concur with the opinion of Paul Farmer, executive director of the American Planning Association, in his column in *Planning*, that "state legislatures are likely to become the new battleground for eminent domain," I am concerned about how planners will respond to this challenge. In delivering customer service, one of the most important factors that determine satisfaction for government services, which is not commonly shared with the delivery of products and services in the private sector, is the customer's perception of fair and equitable treatment. I would argue that a commitment to equity and fairness has been an enduring core value and characteristic of public sector planners. The *Kelo* decision upholds the right of government to violate these core values.

In graduate school in the 1970s, I learned that urban renewal had a dark side. In too many communities, urban renewal became a "black removal" program and it was not just limited to African-Americans. In San Antonio, Hispanic residents were forced out of their marginal businesses and housing for the laudable goals of improving the San Antonio River and spurring economic development. Neighborhoods were removed in Poletown so that General Motors could build a Cadillac plant. Looking back on the history of urban renewal, eminent domain has always been used to promote economic development.

In my opinion, and in the opinion of many Americans, eminent domain should not be commonly and easily used to acquire property for an economic development project from an unwilling seller—especially under the too easily trumped up justifications that are unethically being used to support convenient determinations of blighted property. The primary approach should be for developers, whether from the public or private sector, to negotiate and purchase the property at the cost that is determined by negotiations in the marketplace. Planners have much to gain by not producing bogus determinations of blight and by respecting and upholding the principles of equity and fairness in property transactions that will produce private gains to investors.

In *Kelo*, a majority vote on the Supreme Court concluded that the use of eminent domain for public benefit should be defined and authorized by states and localities. At a minimum, planners should provide leadership for legislative criteria that clearly define and limit the inequitable and unfair use of eminent domain. And planners should be advocates for the establishment of a legislative process that empowers the voters at the state and local levels of government to make these decisions for themselves. Planners would benefit from seeing eminent domain from the perspective of the property owners who now fear their own governments. —*July 27, 2005*

AUTHOR'S UPDATE

On July 26, 2006, the Ohio Supreme Court overturned the use of eminent domain for a redevelopment project in Norwood, Ohio, in *Norwood v. Horney* (161 Ohio App.3d 316 [2006-Ohio-3799]). This was the first major state supreme court case to directly address the issues surrounding those at the core of *Kelo v. City of New London*. The Ohio court ruled that, because of the substantive nature of property rights protections, eminent domain should receive a "higher level of scrutiny" from courts. The unanimous decision of the court specifically invalidated economic development as a sole public purpose that justified using eminent domain. Perhaps more importantly and most relevantly for planning in other states, the Ohio court overturned the blight criteria used to identify redevelopment areas, calling them so vague that they were "standardless standards." Whether the Ohio court decision has a broader impact, and whether other state supreme court decisions such as *Poletown* have had a broader impact, has yet to be seen.

—*September 2006*

BRING SCHOOLS BACK INTO WALKABLE NEIGHBORHOODS

Constance E. Beaumont

School-siting policies and practices work against the concept of community-centered schools.

It startled me when I first heard New Urbanists point out that it's virtually against the law in many parts of this country to build places that people love. But on further reflection, I concluded that they were right. Paris, Charleston, Annapolis, San Francisco, Santa Barbara—these and other beautiful cities treasured for their walkable, intimate streets, their vibrant downtowns, and distinguished architecture, would all flunk the parking, building setback, and other requirements in many zoning laws. Fortunately, local planners all over the United States are reviewing their ordinances with a view to getting rid of provisions that stand in the way of building—or preserving—places that people love.

The same kind of review should occur with respect to rules affecting the location and design of public schools. Thanks to a combination of state policies, local ordinances, and advice handed out by private consultants, it is often difficult to build—or retain—schools that people love—small schools, schools that kids can walk to, schools that tie neighborhoods together, well-designed schools that inspire community pride. Such desirable assets are often inadvertently ruled out by widely applied school facility standards.

Many modern schools have the intimacy and architectural distinction of a Wal-Mart. They are plain, nondescript boxes surrounded by huge parking lots. Their remote locations, large size, and asphalt moats prevent them from being the community-centered schools that so many educators recommend today. Children can't walk to school, and neither can parents or citizens who do volunteer work in our schools.

This is no accident. Misguided policies and practices make it happen.

One problem is the acreage standards applied to many new schools. These typically call for one acre of land for every one hundred students plus ten acres for an elementary school, twenty acres for a middle school, and thirty acres for a high school. In too many cases, school districts must make one of two bad choices in order to satisfy these standards:

- either find a large open space—often a working farm—and then build a "sprawl school" that's physically removed from the community it serves, or

- destroy perfectly good homes near the school to meet the acreage standards.

In Two Rivers, Wisconsin, the school district purchased close to eighty acres of farmland for a new, middle-of-nowhere school while choosing to abandon an in-town school that might have been rehabilitated to meet twenty-first-century standards or replaced with a well-designed new school to which students could have walked. In Mansfield, Ohio, the school district met the state's acreage standards by bulldozing sixty homes in an attractive neighborhood.

The acreage standards are largely intended to ensure that students have plenty of ball fields for sports. But the school-siting decisions necessary to achieve this laudable goal virtually rule out the possibility of walking or biking to school —or to anywhere else after school! As a teenager in Northern Virginia lamented: "If students do any sort of after-school activity, they have to drive themselves home, bum rides, or wait to be picked up. The inconvenience on parents is immense." Fewer than one in eight students walks or bikes to school today.

To its credit, the Council of Educational Facility Planners International recently dropped arbitrary acreage standards from its school planning guide, but these standards (or variations of them) live on in the form of state policies and the mind-sets of many school architects and school district officials.

Policies restricting the amount of money that school districts may invest in the renovation of older schools present another big problem. Under one widely used rule of thumb, if the cost of renovating a school exceeds two-thirds (or some other arbitrary percentage) of the cost of building a new one, the school district is required to build new if it wants state funding assistance. The problem with this rule is that it doesn't consider hidden costs paid by state or local governments. For example, the costs of water and sewer line extensions, student transportation, and roadwork necessary to serve a new school in an outlying area may be ignored. The rule also trivializes long-standing relationships between historic schools and the neighborhoods they've anchored for generations.

A third major problem is the disconnect between land use planning and school facility planning. In many areas, these types of planning occur in separate silos.

It is not uncommon for a town to envision permanent protection for nearby farmland while the school district plans to build new schools, which inevitably attract new residential development, on the same land. Thus land use and school facility planning work at cross-purposes.

A few (though not enough) states are starting to tackle these problems. Maryland, for example, consciously decided not to impose sprawl-promoting acreage standards. The state has worked to maintain prior public investments in schools by favoring maintenance and renovation over the construction of new schools outside smart growth areas.

In Maine, the State Planning Office and Department of Education teamed up to encourage local planning departments and school districts to work together. In a well-illustrated, widely distributed brochure on the "ABCs" of school site-selection, the two agencies recommend locating schools in places that allow kids to walk to school and encouraging school districts to renovate existing schools whenever possible.

In New Jersey and California, school districts must now share their master plans for school construction projects with local government officials. This doesn't guarantee cooperative planning, but it does enhance the prospects for better communication.

Across the country, parents and teachers are clamoring for smaller, more community-centered schools on the grounds that they are better for students and better for learning. It's time for the country as a whole to consider how well-intentioned school-siting policies are undermining that goal. Young people should have the option of walking to a school that anchors a neighborhood. By discarding outdated, arbitrary policies and practices that promote school sprawl—and by pressing for more creative school designs—educators and local officials can help schools reclaim their time-honored role as centers of community.

CONSTANCE E. BEAUMONT

manages education and outreach for the Oregon Transportation and Growth Management Program. She is the author of "Why Johnny Can't Walk to School," an analysis of public policies affecting neighborhood schools published by the National Trust for Historic Preservation.

This article was originally published by Planetizen on January 16, 2002.

RESPONSES FROM READERS

What about the Economics?

While I agree in principle with Ms. Beaumont, I also recognize the economic impact of her argument. Wal-Mart and Target clearly recognize the financial incentives in building fewer, but much larger, "megastores." While many New Urbanists hate these stores, the consumer supports them.

Has any research been done on the economic impact of trying to build, operate, and maintain multiple smaller schools? Each smaller school will still require maintenance staff, a principal, and so forth—costs that would be shared by a larger school.

I do not disagree that smaller, neighborhood-oriented schools might benefit the communities in which they are located for a host of reasons. But what is the opportunity cost to make this policy decision? Perhaps the funds could be more appropriately spent on making larger schools more inviting to the kids they serve?

—January 20, 2002

New Schools, Better Neighborhoods

In California where the need for new school facilities is mammoth (the State Allocation Board estimates that the cost to address our state's pressing school facilities needs is about $40 billion), Constance Beaumont's editorial rings true to those of us working locally and statewide to introduce "New Schools, Better Neighborhoods" principles into our next state school bond.

Given the magnitude of the cost to house our schoolchildren, and the importance of the education mission that the facilities are meant to support, the mission of New Schools Better Neighborhoods (NSBN) to encourage the intelligent joint use of leveraged school, park, health, library, and housing funds has never been more relevant or welcomed. This helps explain why NSBN has been gradually succeeding in promulgating a simple message that portends profound consequences—and possibly a paradigm shift—for how the state funds, and how local school districts think about, the billions of dollars of facilities that we must build to educate California's burgeoning population of school-age children.

The current need to renovate or replace educational facilities presents an opportunity for civic leaders, educators, and community members to take a much smarter view of the design of learning environments. We need to ask how—through creative siting, designing, programming, and joint use with parks, libraries, health care, and other agencies—we can create schools that will serve as centers of communities and neighborhoods that serve as learning environments. This entails designing facilities that can provide direct community access to such spaces as libraries, gymnasiums, auditoriums, performing arts venues, athletic facilities, and recreational spaces that serve the broader needs of the community. It also means intelligently renovating the existing facilities that were and can once again be the anchors of our existing communities.

Yet there is very little attention given to how school facilities can be planned and designed to be effective learning environments. In an attempt to save time and money, districts are sometimes forced to replicate 1950s, suburban, factory-like building plans that are outdated with respect to current educational research and teaching strategies. Consequently, too many of the education facilities being constructed are dinosaurs the day they open.

Still, very real evidence suggests a growing interest in the fusion of smart growth principles with educational and school facilities reform. Legislative leadership is essential if, rather than frustrating efforts to create stronger inner-city and inner-suburban neighborhoods, new school modernization and new facilities monies result in more educational warehouses being built on the fringe of our urban centers.

Our common goal: new schools, better neighborhoods, more livable communities.

—January 20, 2002

AUTHOR'S RESPONSE

Measuring the cost of education by graduates rather than by all students who go through the system suggests that small schools are a wise financial investment, according to an excellent report, *Dollars and Sense: The Cost Effectiveness of Small Schools*, (Cincinnati, OH: KnowledgeWorks Foundation and the Rural School and Community Trust, 2002). Another excellent report, *Smaller, Safer, Saner Successful Schools*, (National Clearing House for Educational Facilities, 2001) observes that "the value of small schools in increasing achievement, graduation rates, satisfaction, and in improving behavior has been confirmed with a clarity and a level of confidence rare in the annals of education research."   *—September 2006*

THE LONE MOUNTAIN COMPACT: A DEBATE ON LIBERTARIAN PLANNING PRINCIPLES

C. Kenneth Orski, G. B. Arrington, Patrick Condon, and John H. Hooker

Participants in an Internet e-mail discussion list engaged in a heated debate in late 2003 on the impact of libertarian principles on urban planning in the United States. Here we present an edited version of the original e-mail debate, which centered on the "Lone Mountain Compact."

The Lone Mountain Compact: Principles for Preserving Freedom and Livability in America's Cities and Suburbs

The phenomenon of urban sprawl has become a preeminent controversy throughout the United States. Recently, a number of scholars and writers, gathered at a conference about the issue at Lone Mountain Ranch in Big Sky, Montana, organized by the Political Economy Research Center. They decided to distill their conclusions into the following brief statement of principles.

Preamble

The unprecedented increase in prosperity over the last twenty-five years has created a large and growing upper middle class in America. New modes of work and leisure combined with population growth have fueled successive waves of suburban expansion in the twentieth century. Technological progress is likely to increase housing choice and community diversity even further in the twenty-first century, enabling more people to live and work outside the conventional urban forms of our time. These choices will likely include low-density, medium-density, and high-density urban forms. This growth brings rapid change to our communities, often with negative side effects, such as traffic congestion, crowded public schools, and the loss of familiar open space. All of these factors are bound up in the controversy that goes by the term "sprawl." The heightened public concern over the character of our cities and suburbs is a healthy expression of citizen demand for solutions that are responsive to our changing needs and wants. Yet tradeoffs between different policy options for addressing these concerns are poorly understood. Productive solutions to public concerns will adhere to the following fundamental principles.

Principles for Livable Cities:

1. The most fundamental principle is that, absent a material threat to other individuals or the community, people should be allowed to live and work where and how they like.

2. Prescriptive, centralized plans that attempt to determine the detailed outcome of community form and function should be avoided. Such "comprehensive" plans interfere with the dynamic, adaptive, and evolutionary nature of neighborhoods and cities.

3. Densities and land uses should be market driven, not plan driven. Proposals to supersede market-driven land use decisions by centrally directed decisions are vulnerable to the same kind of perverse consequences as any other kind of centrally planned resource allocation decisions, and show little awareness of what such a system would have to accomplish even to equal the market in effectiveness.

4. Communities should allow a diversity in neighborhood design, as desired by the market. Planning and zoning codes and building regulations should allow for neotraditional neighborhood design, historic neighborhood renovation and conversion, and other mixed-use development and the more decentralized development forms of recent years.

5. Decisions about neighborhood development should be decentralized as far as possible. Local neighborhood associations and private covenants are superior to centralized or regional government planning agencies.

6. Local planning procedures and tools should incorporate private property rights as a fundamental element of development control. Problems of incompatible or conflicting land uses will be better resolved through the revival of common law principles of nuisance than through zoning regulations which tend to be rigid and inefficient.

7. All growth management policies should be evaluated according to their cost of living and "burden-shifting" effects. Urban growth boundaries, minimum lot sizes,

restrictions on housing development, restrictions on commercial development, and other limits on freely functioning land markets that increase the burdens on lower income groups must be rejected.

8. Market-oriented transportation strategies should be employed, such as peak-period road pricing, HOT lanes, toll roads, and de-monopolized mass transit. Monopoly public transit schemes, especially fixed rail transit that lacks the flexibility to adapt to the changing destinations of a dynamic, decentralized metropolis, should be viewed skeptically.

9. The rights of present residents should not supersede those of future residents. Planners, citizens, and local officials should recognize that "efficient" land use must include consideration for household and consumer wants, preferences, and desires. Thus, growth controls and land-use planning must consider the desires of future residents and generations, not solely current residents.

10. Planning decisions should be based upon facts, not perceptions. A number of the concerns raised in the "sprawl" debate are based upon false perceptions. The use of good data in public policy is crucial to the continued progress of American cities and the social advance of all its citizens.

Kenneth Orski

The Lone Mountain Compact (of which I am proud to be a signatory) is a collection of principles, the key of which is that people ought to be allowed to live and work where and how they choose. However, to characterize the Lone Mountain Coalition as "Libertarian" is a misnomer. The Lone Mountain Coalition has no political agenda. It is a group of like-minded individuals who believe in limited government, maximum individual freedom, and market-driven land use decisions.

G. B. Arrington

You submitted the Lone Mountain Compact as an illustration of the principles you would apply to a site. New Urbanism is all about creating wonderful, vibrant places for people. For the New Urbanist place, design and the interaction of uses matter. For the Lone Mountain gang, it appears what matters most is the absence of government, and the ability to make decisions unfettered by others. I'm sure you will politely disagree. So in the defense of your compact, I'd love to have you forward the site plans and renderings of a community that you feel embraces and follows the Lone Mountain Compact, along with a short explanation of how the compact has been applied to create a great and wonderful place that we would want to include at the Congress for New Urbanism.

Kenneth Orski

I have no quarrel with New Urbanism and its desire to create livable places through rational planning and more attractive design. I have always been a great admirer of Andrés Duany and his followers, and I subscribe to the principles they stand for. My quarrel (if I may call it that) is with the smart growth movement, which is not a set of planning or design principles but rather a political ideology with an authoritarian bent—an ideology that is at odds with the principles of free choice and decentralized decision making that I believe both New Urbanism and the Lone Mountain Compact stand for. Let us once and for all distinguish between New Urbanism and smart growth. By so doing, I think we shall avoid a lot of future misunderstandings.

Patrick Condon

Yes, let us distinguish between New Urbanist principles deployed at the site scale, where they might lead to an attractive, livable, but atypical community (an activity that Mr. Orski seems to support), and any attempt to encourage the broader community of citizens to also enjoy these advantages (an activity that Mr. Orski opposes). There is a huge difference between democracy and "authoritarianism." It is shameful to confuse them.

John Hooker

Some thoughts in response to the Lone Mountain Compact itself: Is zoning "prescriptive and centralized"? Most public planning today consists of amendments to zoning maps and the ongoing redefinition of public rights-of-way. Are ad hoc private government and zoning superior to established public processes?

Is the market always free of perverse consequences as it maximizes individual (and corporate) benefits regardless of public costs? How will public infrastructure be planned and funded if changes in existing densities are dynamic and decentralized? What do we do with overcapacity and long-term public debt when the density does not occur or the uses leave? Are impact fees an undue burden on the market and the poor?

Do private landowners really want to fight every battle with their neighbors, new and old, over alleged nuisances in an unregulated land use market? Is there a limit to dynamism?

How do the signers define "efficient" land use? What are "growth controls"? How far into the future should we plan? Who will do that planning for the future, especially if all decisions are made at the neighborhood level?

Are the parties even ready to agree on the "facts" at all? For example, Smart Growth America produced a survey of some fifty-odd metropolitan areas and ranked them regarding "sprawl" by a large set of criteria. Supporters of the status quo will selectively choose the specific criteria that support the argument that their town is not "sprawling." Another example is the arguments over global warming and the generation of greenhouse gases. Then there is the challenge of the enormous "ecological footprints" that our dynamic, decentralized metropolises demand. There is some debate about how sustainable this lifestyle is. How will the market of today respond to the potential disasters of tomorrow?

Kenneth Orski

We could go on forever arguing the finer points of the free market versus government intervention. But that misses my original point—that New Urbanism should not be confused with the smart growth movement. The former is a laudable effort to make our urban and suburban communities more livable, a goal that I and my colleagues in the Lone Mountain Compact community share.

Smart growth is a movement with a political agenda that has nothing to do with improving people's daily lives. Rather, it is an effort by a certain group of urban elitists to impose their lifestyle choices on the vast majority of Americans who prefer a suburban lifestyle—and, in the guise of "sprawl containment" and "open space preservation"—deprive low-income households of an opportunity to share in the American dream of home ownership.

G. B. Arrington

I would add that nowhere in the "debate" does Mr. Orski ever provide an example of a built project reflecting libertarian principles. To be useful we need to move beyond theory and look at what is happening in the built world. The real difference between libertarians and New Urbanists is that the New Urbanists are engaged in the practical work of building and planning projects. If the libertarians want to be taken seriously in the debate on planning, they need to move out of ivory towers and into the real world, where the action is.

C. KENNETH ORSKI

is the editor and publisher of *Innovation Briefs*.

G.B. ARRINGTON

is the senior professional associate for transit-oriented development at the Parsons Brinckerhoff Land Use Resource Center in Portland, Oregon.

PATRICK CONDON

is the James Taylor Chair in Landscape and Livable Environments at the University of British Columbia.

JOHN HOOKER

is the former mayor of the Village of Los Ranchos de Albuquerque, New Mexico.

This article was originally published by Planetizen on January 19, 2004.

RESPONSES FROM READERS

Time for a Reality Check?

I commiserate with landowners who decry the ulterior motives of upper-middle-class suburbanites and rural settlers who push for "concurrent" development and wave "green" flags to gate their communities, but let's now be honest on both sides. The Lone Mountain principles might work if only roads were naturally occurring phenomena that fluctuated with traffic congestion; abundant fresh water was universally available just below ground; humans did not generate unhealthful waste; trees were mere lawn ornaments; all emergency services were voluntary; and light, noise, odor, and vibration were dissolved by property boundaries.

Tax-and-spend libertarians would apparently have your tax dollars extend unlimited road capacity to every corner of the country, absorb virtually unlimited costs of environmental cleanup (including underutilized roads), and provide pro bono representation for all nuisance claims. Businesslike, efficient provision of public infrastructure and services, in part through impact (user) fees for capital facilities; consumer choice of transportation mode; proactive environmental impact mitigation; and assurances of freedom for one to enjoy use of one's land without encroachment by one's neighbor are in fact smart.

—January 23, 2004

Democracy Versus Authoritarianism

It is apparent from the exchange between Orski and Arrington that New Urbanism reflects both of their points of view. The difference is about how and whether or not regulating a better tomorrow is either democracy or authoritarianism. Mr. Orski feels it is the latter and wants development to be unfettered by regulation of any sort. While regulation has not produced wonderful results, no regulation of any sort is bound to either repeat the past or make it worse in the present.

Economic development is more than just civic aesthetics. It is about being able to predict the cost and timing of providing supporting public infrastructure and services. I think it would be a good idea if Mr. Orski just dropped his ideological template by which he measures the consistency of smart growth and government regulation to the Lone Mountain Compact and consider what kind of future is preferable for cities, the environment, and the people who live in it.

Clearly, when folks have to deal with bad economic development, they are not relieved to know whether Mr. Orski's or New Urbanism's or smart growth's programs were guiding principles. This should not be a fight about ideologies when the future and how it is guided to everyone's benefit is the real and only issue.

—January 22, 2004

Smart Growth Is an Ideology

The problem with New Urbanism is *not* the design of these communities, or zoning ordinances, but when they become so embraced by politicians and planners as *the* solution to all of our ills. In my view, smart growth should be about restoring and revitalizing existing cities and suburbs—not downzoning farmers, depriving suburbanites of new highways, or stipulating that one way of design is the only way.

Unfortunately, this type of "snob growth" has become a convenient weapon to use against people who want a low-density suburban lifestyle or for politicians to justify billions for light and heavy rail projects over multimodal highways. So, Ken is right. Smart growth is an ideology, and the Lone Mountain principles are what we need to foster in this country—not heavy-handed, coercive zoning masquerading as "smart growth" or smart whatever.

—January 22, 2004

EDITORS

Abhijeet Chavan is the co–founder and co–editor in chief of Planetizen. He is also the chief technology officer of Urban Insight Inc. Abhijeet previously served as the information technology coordinator for the East St. Louis Action Research Project, a service learning initiative of the University of Illinois at Urbana-Champaign (UIUC) for revitalizing distressed urban communities. He also coordinated geographic data visualization projects at UIUC's Imaging Systems Laboratory.

Christian Peralta became managing editor of Planetizen in 2006 after having contributed significantly to its development as an associate editor from 2000 to 2003. Before rejoining the Planetizen team, he spent almost two years living and working in Asia, serving as a program manager at the China Planning and Development Institute. Christian previously worked as a policy analyst at Livable Places, a Los Angeles–based nonprofit organization working to promote sustainable development.

Christopher Steins is the co–founder and co–editor-in-chief of Planetizen. He is also the chief executive of Urban Insight Inc., the Internet consulting firm that operates Planetizen. Chris was formerly the managing editor of *The Planning Report* and *Metro Investment Report*, two Los Angeles–based trade monthlies reporting on urban planning, real estate, and infrastructure development. He previously served as the executive director of a Los Angeles–based nonprofit affordable housing development corporation involved in public–private joint venture development.

CONTRIBUTORS

G. B. Arrington is senior professional associate for transit-oriented development at the Parsons Brinckerhoff Land Use Resource Center in Portland, Oregon.

Constance E. Beaumont manages education and outreach for the Oregon Transportation and Growth Management Program. She is the author of "Why Johnny Can't Walk to School," an analysis of public policies affecting neighborhood schools published by the National Trust for Historic Preservation.

Edward J. Blakely was dean of the Robert J. Milano Graduate School in New York City at the time of his article in this volume. He is a fellow of the National Academy of Public Administration and was previously dean of the School of Urban Planning and Development at the University of Southern California in Los Angeles. Blakely also served as the chair of city and regional planning at the University of California at Berkeley, where he assisted the City of Oakland recovery efforts from both the earthquake in 1989 and the fires in 1991. He is the author of *Fortress America: Gated Communities in the United States* (Thousand Oaks, CA: Brookings Institution Press, 1997) and the co-author of *Fundamentals of Economic Development Finance* (Sage, 2001). He is now professor of urban planning at the University of Sydney and continues to be engaged in city rebuilding in New Orleans, Asia, and Australia.

Dan Burden is a nationally recognized authority on bicycle and pedestrian facilities and programs. He has had twenty-seven years of experience in developing, promoting, and evaluating alternative transportation facilities, traffic-calming practices, and sustainable community design. He served for sixteen years as the Florida Department of Transportation's state bicycle and pedestrian coordinator, and he currently is executive director of Walkable Communities Inc., a nonprofit corporation helping North America develop walkable communities, and a partner with Glatting Jackson.

Thomas J. Campanella is assistant professor of urban design and city planning at the University of North Carolina at Chapel Hill and a visiting professor at Nanjing University's Graduate School of Architecture. He co-edited *The Resilient City: How Modern Cities Recover from Disaster* (New York: Oxford University Press, 2005) with Lawrence J. Vale of the Massachusetts Institute of Technology.

Patrick Condon is the James Taylor Chair in Landscape and Livable Environments at the University of British Columbia.

Wendell Cox is principal of Wendell Cox Consultancy, an international public policy firm. He has provided consulting assistance to the United States Department of Transportation and is a visiting professor at the Conservatoire National des Arts et Metiers in Paris. He has consulted for public transit authorities in the United States, Canada, Australia, and New Zealand and for public policy organizations.

Christopher DeWolf lives in Montreal, where he is a writer, a photographer, and the editor of Urbanphoto.net, a website dedicated to exploring the urban environment through photography.

Andrés Duany, FAIA, is a principal of Duany Plater-Zyberk & Company. He is a co-founder and member of the Congress for the New Urbanism.

Anthony Flint is a former reporter for *The Boston Globe* and the author of *This Land: The Battle Over Sprawl and the Future of America*, published in April 2006 by Johns Hopkins University Press. He is currently public affairs manager for the Lincoln Institute of Land Policy, a think tank based in Cambridge, Massachusetts, where he continues to write about land and development. His forthcoming book on Jane Jacobs and Robert Moses in New York in the 1960s will be published in 2008 by Random House.

William Fulton is president of Solimar Research Group and editor and publisher of *California Planning & Development Report,* author of *Guide to California Planning* (2nd ed., Baltimore, MD: Solano Press Books, 1999) and *The Reluctant Metropolis: The Politics of Urban Growth in Los Angeles* (Johns Hopkins University Press, 2001), and co-author with Peter Calthorpe of *The Regional City: Planning for the End of Sprawl* (Washington, D.C.: Island Press, 2001).

Alexander Garvin has combined a career in urban planning and real estate with teaching, architecture, and public service. He is currently president and CEO of Alex Garvin & Associates Inc. He was managing director of Planning for NYC2012, New York City's committee for the 2012 Olympic bid, and was vice president for planning, design, and development at the Lower Manhattan Development Corporation, the agency charged with the redevelopment of the World Trade Center following 9/11. Over the past thirty-five years, Mr. Garvin held prominent positions in five New York City administrations, including deputy commissioner of housing and city planning commissioner. He is a professor of urban planning and management at Yale University, where he has taught for thirty-nine years.

John Hooker is former mayor of the Village of Los Ranchos de Albuquerque, New Mexico.

Fred Kent is president of Project for Public Spaces in New York and a leading authority on revitalizing city spaces.

Joel Kotkin is an Irvine Senior Fellow with the New America Foundation. He is also the author of *The City: A Global History* (New York: Modern Library, 2005). He is currently writing a book on the American Future for Penguin Books.

Kenneth E. Kruckemeyer is a transportation strategist in Boston and can be reached via the internet at kek@mit.edu.

James Howard Kunstler is the author of four books: *The Geography of Nowhere* (New York: Simon and Schuster, 1993), *Home from Nowhere* (New York: Simon and Schuster, 1996), *The City in Mind: Notes on the Urban Condition* (New York: Free Press, 2001), and *The Long Emergency* (New York: Atlantic Monthly Press, 2005). He lives in Saratoga Springs, New York.

Michael Mehaffy is a project manager, urban designer, and educator as well as president of Structura Naturalis Inc., an urban design and consulting firm based in Portland, Oregon.

John Norquist is the former mayor of Milwaukee and the author of the book *The Wealth of Cities* (Reading, MA: Perseus Books, 1998). He also serves as president of the Congress for the New Urbanism, which hosts an annual Congress.

Robert B. Olshansky is professor of urban and regional planning at the University of Illinois at Urbana-Champaign. His teaching and research cover land use and environmental planning, with an emphasis on planning for natural hazards.

C. Kenneth Orski is editor and publisher of *Innovation Briefs*.

Randal O'Toole, an economist with the Thoreau Institute, organized the "Preserving the American Dream" conference held in Washington, D.C., in February 2003. An Oregon native, he has lived most of his life in Portland but currently lives in Bandon, Oregon.

Neal Peirce is chairman of the Citistates Group, a network of journalists, speakers and civic leaders focused on building competitive, equitable and sustainable 21st century metropolitan regions. His weekly syndicated column on emerging trends in local and state government is distributed by the Washington Post Writers Group; interested readers can also sign up to receive it by e-mail at www.citistates.com/np_columns.html.

Nikos A. Salingaros, MA, PhD, ICTP, is a world-respected urbanist and architectural theorist. He is professor of mathematics at the University of Texas at San Antonio and is concurrently on the architecture faculties of the universities of Rome III, Delft, and Querétaro, Mexico. He has written three books: *Principles of Urban Structure* (Amsterdam, Techne Press, 2005), *A Theory of Architecture* (Solingen, Umbau-Verlag, 2006), and *Anti-Architecture and Deconstruction* (Solingen, Umbau-Verlag, 2004).

Peter Samuel is editor of *TOLLROADSnews* (www.tollroadsnews.com) and a senior fellow in transportation studies at Reason Foundation in Los Angeles, CA. He has taught economics and written for newspapers and magazines on various public policy issues. In the past twelve years, he has specialized in writing about tollroads and road pricing. Of British and Australian extraction, he has been in the Washington, D.C., metro area for the past twenty-four years.

Charles Shaw is a writer and activist living in Chicago. He is editor-in-chief of *Conscious Choice*, senior staff writer and development editor for *The Next American City*, and a regular contributor to *Alternet, Grist, In These Times, Scoop,* and the *Guerrilla News Network*.

Donald C. Shoup, FAICP, is professor of urban planning at the University of California, Los Angeles and has written many books and papers on parking, including *The High Cost of Free Parking* (Planners Press, 2005), a Planetizen Top Book for 2005, which explains the theory and practice of parking management.

Jeff Speck, a city planner, was director of design at the National Endowment for the Arts, where he oversaw the Mayors' Institute on City Design until stepping down in May 2007. He is co-author with Andrés Duany and Elizabeth Plater-Zyberk of *Suburban Nation: The Rise of Sprawl and the Decline of the American Dream* (New York: North Point Press, 2000).

Samuel R. Staley, directs urban and land use policy at Reason Foundation (a nonprofit think tank based in Los Angeles), teaches urban economics at the University of Dayton, and is former chair of his local planning board (in Bellbrook, Ohio). He has written more than one hundred articles, reports, and studies on urban policy and planning. His most recent books include *The Road More Traveled: Why the Congestion Crisis Matters More Than You Think and What We Can Do About It* (New York: Rowman and Littlefield, 2006) and *Smarter Growth: Market-based Strategies for Land-use Planning in the 21st Century* (Westport, CT: Greenwood Press, 2001).

Harriet Tregoning is director of the Office of Planning for the District of Columbia. Prior to this she was the Director of the Governors' Institute on Community Design and executive director of the Smart Growth Leadership Institute (a project of the national nonprofit advocacy organization Smart Growth America). She is the former secretary of planning and former secretary for smart growth for Maryland. While at the United States Environmental Protection Agency, she founded the National Smart Growth Network, a national partnership program designed to inform and accelerate innovative smart growth policies and practices.

Michael Woo was the first trained urban planner elected to serve on the Los Angeles City Council, on which he chaired the Transportation and Traffic Committee and was a member of the Planning and Land Use Management Committee. He currently serves as one of Mayor Antonio Villaraigosa's appointees to the Los Angeles City Planning Commission and is board chairman of Smart Growth America. Woo teaches urban planning at the University of Southern California and, at the University of California, Los Angeles, a special course on sustainable development in China.

INDEX

ISLAND PRESS BOARD OF DIRECTORS

Victor M. Sher, Esq. *(Chair)*
Sher & Leff
San Francisco, CA

Dane A. Nichols *(Vice-Chair)*
Washington, DC

Carolyn Peachey *(Secretary)*
Campbell, Peachey & Associates
Washington, DC

Drummond Pike *(Treasurer)*
President
The Tides Foundation
San Francisco, CA

Robert Baensch
Director, Center for Publishing
New York University
New York, NY

William H. Meadows
President
The Wilderness Society
Washington, DC

Merloyd Ludington Lawrence
Merloyd Lawrence Inc.
Boston, MA

Henry Reath
Princeton, NJ

Will Rogers
President
The Trust for Public Land
San Francisco, CA

Alexis G. Sant
Trustee and Treasurer
Summit Foundation
Washington, DC

Charles C. Savitt
President
Island Press
Washington, DC

Susan E. Sechler
Senior Advisor
The German Marshall Fund
Washington, DC

Nancy Sidamon-Eristoff
Washington, DC

Peter R. Stein
General Partner
LTC Conservation Advisory Services
The Lyme Timber Company
Hanover, NH

Diana Wall, Ph.D.
Director and Professor
Natural Resource Ecology Laboratory
Colorado State University
Fort Collins, CO

Wren Wirth
Washington, DC